CREATING Books & BOXES

QUARRY

GLOUCESTER MASSACHUSETTS

CREATING
Books
& BOXES

Fun and Unique Approaches to Handmade Structures

QUARRY BOOKS

BENJAMIN D. RINEHART

First published in the United States of America by

Quarry Books, a member of
Quayside Publishing Group
33 Commercial Street
Gloucester, Massachusetts 01930-5089
Telephone: (978) 282-9590
Fax: (978) 283-2742
www.rockpub.com

Library of Congress Cataloging-in-Publication Data

Rinehart, Benjamin D.
  Creating books and boxes : fun and unique approaches to handmade structures /
Benjamin D. Rinehart.
      p. cm.
  ISBN 1-59253-291-8 (pbk.)
  1. Bookbinding. 2. Book design. 3. Box making. I. Title.
Z271.R56 2006
686.3—dc22

2006019004
CIP

ISBN-13: 978-1-59253-291-9
ISBN-10: 1-59253-291-8

10 9 8 7 6 5 4 3 2 1

Design: Laura H. Couallier, Laura Herrmann Design
Cover Image: Allan Penn
Templates and Illustrations: Benjamin D. Rinehart

Printed in Singapore

Contents

Preface

MY PASSION FOR MAKING ART BEGAN at an early age. My parents encouraged my creativity by enrolling me for classes in painting, drawing, and anything else that was available in our hometown. I kept myself busy as a child by drawing and creating imaginary creatures in my sketchbook.

Drawing continued to be a strong focus for me throughout high school and college and eventually led me to printmaking. From that point, it was a natural step to begin incorporating my printed images into various book formats. I have worked consistently with the figure in my artwork, creating narratives about family, friends, and myself. My desire for learning new bookmaking and printmaking processes is sustained by the challenges they afford; it is the wonderful novelty that keeps me interested in making art.

A problem solver by nature, it is my passion as an educator to inform and assist each student in finding the best possible solution for achieving his or her artistic goals. My belief is that whatever I learn I should share with others, and in turn my mentors, colleagues, peers, and students continue to be an indispensable resource of knowledge and inspiration.

Introduction

BOOKS ENCOMPASS MANY DIFFERENT ideas. When I think of a book, sequence and narration come to mind. Any artwork that deals with text and/or image in this manner is a book to me. A deck of cards is just as much a book as a sculpture made of binder's board and book cloth.

My idea of what makes a book a book is quite liberal. And there are many different types of books to consider: accordions, pop-ups, pamphlets, side stitches, altered books, portfolios, boxes, tunnel books, and puzzle books, to name just a few. Can sculpture be a book? Can a painting or box? Sure! Come up with your own definition, but in the end, make wonderful artwork!

With that said, making books and boxes does not have to be intimidating. This book examines terminology, tools, and materials, and includes step-by-step projects with variations along with helpful tips on each structure. *Creating Books and Boxes* is a compilation of much of the content that I have created and used for my classes and workshops. The classroom has been a great way for my students to get to know the material and become comfortable with folding, cutting, sewing, and gluing—the essentials in book and box making—but you don't need to take a class to learn the basics and make wonderful works of art.

My goal is that this book will serve as a literal and visual guide to making your own beautiful bound and boxed creations. Enjoy yourself and keep in mind that when learning something new, mistakes happen. Embrace this, because it will only make you a better artist and craftsperson. Be brave and experiment with different materials and forms. I hope that you find the projects in this book insightful, captivating, and fun!

Note: All measurements are in inches and metric. However, you'll probably find the metric system to be more accurate and less confusing than converting fractions. Give it a try!

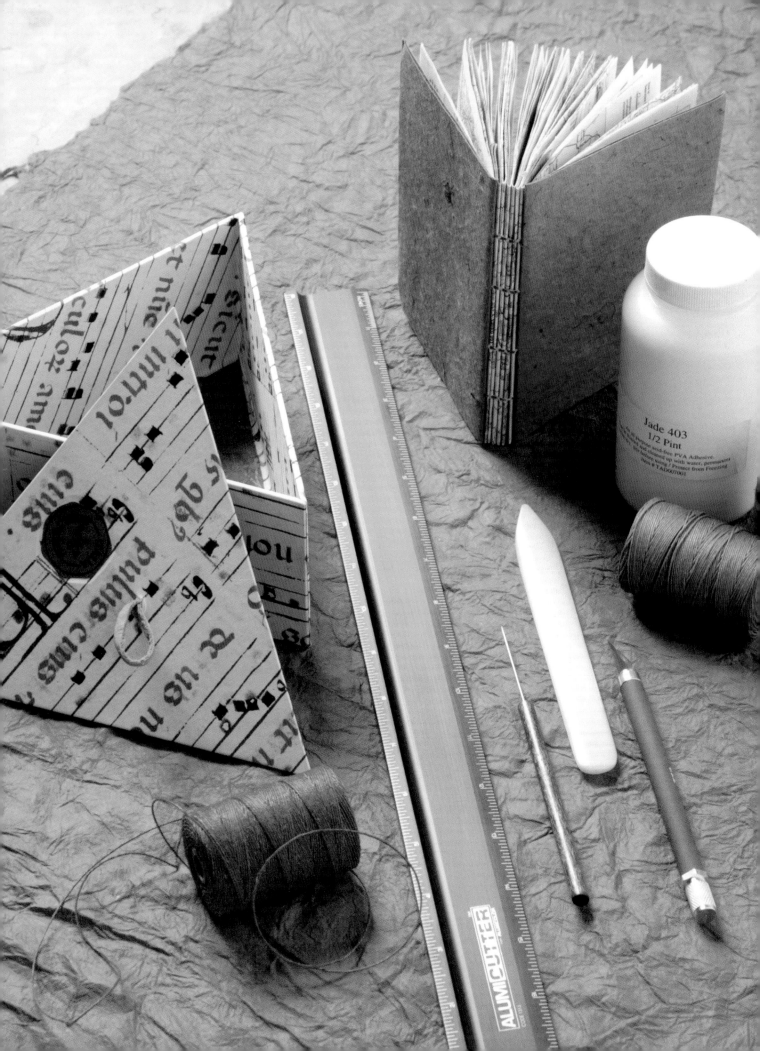

Essentials

1

THIS SECTION COVERS ALL OF THE background information necessary to complete each project. I recommend going through each section to gain greater insight into each project. Even the experienced bookbinder is *bound* to pick up a few new tricks.

The first three topics include basic book terms, the tools required for the projects, and archival materials. What follows are basic bookbinding methods such as testing for grain direction, squaring and cutting materials, creating torn edges, trimming text blocks, folding and scoring, and sewing—including preparation of the signatures to connecting separate threads. The adhesives section will help you learn why and how certain adhesives are used and provide you with some valuable recipes. Final topics include gluing the materials, tipping on panels, turning over edges, adding corner options and most important—keeping the projects flat.

BOOKBINDING TERMS

BOOKBINDERS, CONSERVATORS, artists, and writers commonly use the following terms. Some terms may vary slightly in different regions, so do not be surprised if you encounter variations.

HEAD: top side of the book

TAIL or FOOT: bottom side of the book

SPINE: back side of the book; gives flexibility and support

FOREDGE: side of the book that opens

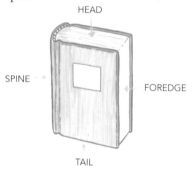

TEXT BLOCK: pages or the inside of the book

SQUARE: extra space around the edges of the cover; designed to protect the text block

END SHEET, END PAPER, or FLY LEAF: sheet that attaches the text block to the cover or a sheet to cover the turnovers

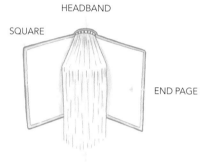

HEADBAND: decoration and added support for the text block

PAGE: one side of the leaf

LEAF: single sheet of paper or one-half of a folio (equals two pages)

FOLIO: single sheet folded in half (equals four pages)

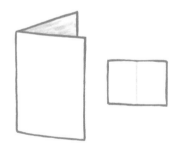

QUARTO: single sheet folded twice (equals eight pages); may be used as a self-contained signature

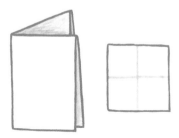

OCTAVO: single sheet folded three times (equals sixteen pages); may be used as a self-contained signature

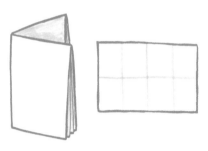

SIGNATURE or SECTION: gathering of folios; a quarto or octavo

PEAK: top folded edge of a piece of paper

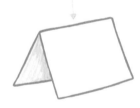

GUTTER or VALLEY: inside of the folded edge of a piece of paper

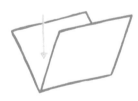

SEWING STATIONS: holes created through which to sew

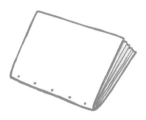

TOOLS

BELOW ARE THE BASIC TOOLS needed for each project. Keep in mind that many household items may be substituted in a number of ways to aid in construction. As an example, the butter knife may be used instead of the bone folder for folding, scoring, and tearing open pages. Many of these tools can be found at art, hardware, or specialty bookbinding supply stores (see Suppliers & Resources, page 140).

(a) BONE FOLDER: The primary tool used for folding, scoring, and tearing paper.

(b) BUTTER KNIFE or LETTER OPENER: These tools are used for tearing paper and scoring. A non-serrated butter knife is preferred to minimize excessive tearing or chewing of the paper.

(c) PENCIL: A mechanical pencil is recommended because the lead is always sharp.

(d) WHITE PLASTIC ERASER: A great eraser to use because it erases cleanly and does not mark up the surface of the materials.

(e) RUBBER CEMENT PICK-UP ERASER: This eraser helps remove dried adhesive from the paper and cloth.

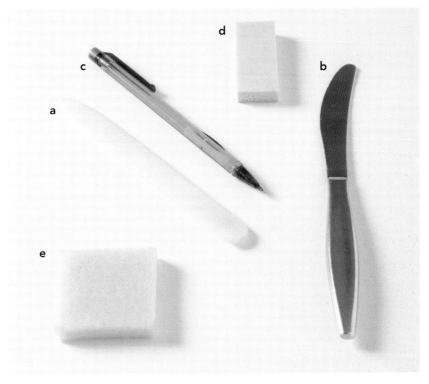

(Note: f through j shown on page 14.)

(f) METAL RULER: An 18" (45.7 cm) or longer ruler is recommended. A thicker ruler without a cork backing ensures that the materials rest neatly against the straight edge.

(g) TRIANGLES: Used for mitering corners and for right angles. Both 45/45/90- and 30/60/90-degree triangles are recommended. Metal triangles are more durable than plastic, but a plastic triangle with a metal edge works just as well.

(h) SCISSORS: A good sharp pair of scissors is necessary and helpful for most projects.

(i) CUTTING MAT: Also known as a *self-healing* or *quilter's* mat. This is a wonderful surface on which to cut and fold. A scrap piece of cardboard may be substituted. An 18" × 24" (45.7 × 61 cm) or larger mat is recommended to create a large enough work space.

(j) CRAFT KNIFE: A pencil-shaped tool with replaceable blades used for cutting thin or delicate materials. This is preferred over a scalpel because the blades are easier to acquire and replace.

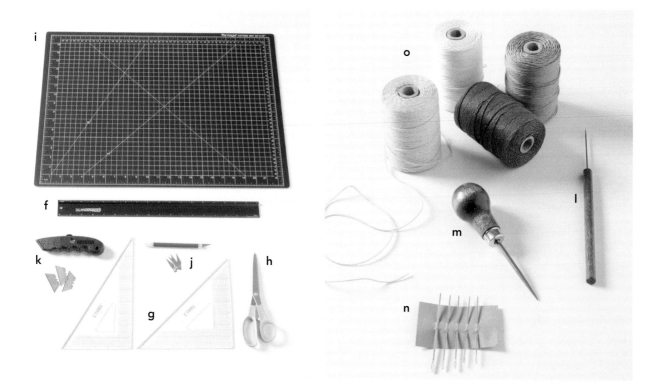

(k) UTILITY or MAT KNIFE: This handheld tool is used for cutting heavier materials. The blades are retractable and replaceable. A heavier utility knife with snap-off blades may also be used.

(l) PIN TOOL: Used for punching sewing stations or smaller holes. This tool is the same as a ceramic potter's needle, although the thickness may vary. It is known as a small bookbinder's awl.

(m) AWL: Used for punching sewing stations or larger holes through heavier materials. this tool has a fatter post than the pin tool.

(n) TAPESTRY, UPHOLSTERY, or DARNER'S NEEDLES: These needles are ideal because the eye of the needle is not much larger than the post, which keeps the sewing stations from tearing or ripping during sewing. A variety of sizes are available. The needle should be a similar thickness to the thread to minimize tearing while sewing.

(o) LINEN THREAD: This special thread is strong, archival, and comes in a variety of colors.

(p) ARTIST'S TAPE: This tape is great to have around to temporarily tape two surfaces together. Painter's or artist's tape is typically white or blue. These are preferred to masking tape, because they are normally archival and have less tack or sticking power so the surface does not become damaged.

(q) GLUE BRUSHES: Several sizes of brushes are helpful. They come in a variety of widths: ½", 1", and 2" (1.3, 2.5, and 5.1 cm). Inexpensive horsehair bristle brushes work well.

(r) POLYVINYL ACETATE (PVA): A strong adhesive used to glue heavier materials together. It is similar in appearance to school glue.

(s) METHYL CELLULOSE: A lighter weight adhesive found in powder form. This paste is easy to mix and may be used alone or mixed with the PVA.

PLASTIC CONTAINERS (not shown): Any plastic containers may be used to hold adhesive mixtures. A snap-on lid is helpful to keep the adhesive from drying out.

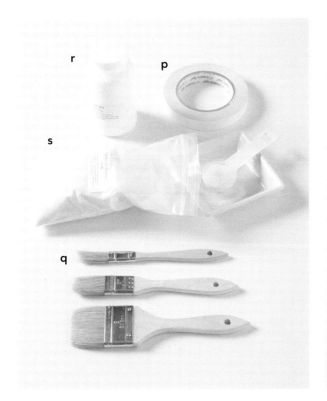

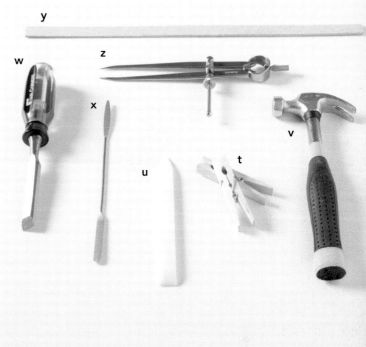

WAX PAPER (not shown): Any regular brand is helpful when constructing boxes and gluing spines. The adhesives do not stick to the waxed surface of the paper.

WASTE PAPER (not shown): Any scrap paper may be used for gluing the projects. Avoid newspapers and ink-jet printouts because the moisture in the adhesive may cause the ink to bleed onto the glued surface. A clean newsprint tablet is ideal because it tears off easily and is inexpensive.

BOARDS (not shown): Wooden boards are used for weighting and pressing the projects. Boards measuring 9" × 12" (22.9 × 30.5 cm) or larger are ideal. Any flat surface may be substituted as long as it is larger than the project.

WEIGHTS (not shown): Weights are used to apply pressure after gluing to ensure that the project does not warp or buckle. A wide variety of heavy things may be used, including bricks, metal, or books.

(t) **CLOTHESPINS:** Used to hold sheets of paper together. The clothespins function as an extra pair of hands that do not damage the materials like heavier clips.

(u) **TEFLON FOLDER:** A plastic tool that may be used instead of a bone folder. Great for making boxes and magically does not mark up the surface of the paper, cloth, or board like the bone folder.

(v) **HAMMER:** A hammer is helpful when using an awl or chisel. It may also be used to flatten raised materials.

(w) **CHISEL:** A useful tool to punch through heavier materials and to create slits for ribbons. A variety of sizes may be purchased at a hardware store. Chisels measuring ¼" and ½" (6 mm and 1.3 cm) wide are good sizes to have at hand.

(x) **MICRO-SPATULA:** Used for tearing and for pushing materials through slender areas and other hard-to-get-at places.

(y) **CHEATER'S STRIP:** A metal strip may be purchased from a hardware store in a standard thickness of ⅝" (1.5 cm). This is ideal for turn-ins and holds up well to cutting when used as a straight edge. A cheaper version made of scrap binder's board works just as well.

(z) **SPRING DIVIDER:** A device used to measure precise distances. This small caliper minimizes the need for a ruler.

ARCHIVAL MATERIALS

WHEN MAKING BOOKS AND boxes, use materials that do not contain acid to maintain a neutral pH balance. Acid causes natural materials such as cotton, wood, and even metal to rot or oxidize. Newspapers are a prime example of what can happen over an extended period of time. The yellowing of the newspaper is the acid eroding the fibers of the paper, causing it to become brittle and eventually fall apart. Even using a nonarchival material with something that is archival causes the acid from the nonarchival material to leech onto the good material. This drastically shortens the life of the book.

Along with the paper, board, and cloth, adhesives should also have a neutral pH. The adhesives commonly used have either a synthetic or natural base.

Polyvinyl acetate (PVA) and methyl cellulose are two of the most commonly used adhesives and are consistently acid free (see Adhesives, page 30). The glue container should list the archival properties.

Paper treatments such as oils and wax may introduce foreign acidic elements to the materials and cause damage. Even ink from a computer printer may not be archival. If the archival information is not listed on the product, contact the company or distributor before using.

Ideally a book should last well past the lifetime of the artist or author. Paying attention to the properties of the materials lengthens the life of the book, giving many generations the pleasure that was intended.

Once the archival quality has been determined for each material, another important aspect is to gain a greater sensitivity to the materials. When choosing materials, trust the sense of touch to determine the appropriate thickness and surface quality in relation to the project. Experience with the materials and how they react to folding, sewing, cutting, and gluing comes with time. Make a note of the materials used for each project to compare their individual characteristics. The following describes some of the different materials used in book and box making.

TIP A special pen may be purchased at an art supply or framing store to test the acidity level of each product. This is helpful when no information is available about the material.

PAPER

Text Weight Paper – A light to medium weight paper that is ideal for printing, writing, or sketching. The paper's weight is determined in pounds or grams. Text weight paper is most similar to copy or printer paper. Any paper that is thinner could also be considered a text weight paper. These papers fold and cut more easily than cover weight paper or board. The weight of the paper is typically 70 lb (105.4 gsm) or less.

Cover Weight Paper – Cover paper is used for covers and end sheets. It is typically medium to heavy weight. Depending on the thickness, thin bristol board could also be considered a heavy cover weight paper. Folding and cutting cover weight papers requires more effort. The weight of the paper is typically 70 lb (105.4 gsm) or more.

Tissue Paper – This paper may be used in a number of ways. It is chosen for projects because of its strength and varied surfaces. When the paper is dampened or glued it becomes increasingly delicate to the touch; when dry, however, it is typically stronger than most text weight papers. Tissue paper may be used as pages, spine linings, inner bindings, and paper dyeing to name just a few.

BOARD

Binder's Board – A wonderful sturdy board used primarily in book and box making. The board comes in a variety of sizes: .067", .082", and .098" (1.7, 2.1, and 2.5 mm). A medium weight board is a great starting point. Because the board is processed in layers, insets for covers and channels for ribbons are easy to cut. The board has metal fragments combined with the paper pulp during production, making it more difficult to cut through. A heavier utility knife with a sharp blade makes the job a little easier. Binder's board is typically gray in appearance and is not the same as the cardboard found on the back of paper tablets. The board used commercially as a backing is called *chipboard* and is typically not archival. Even some binder's board is not archival, so be mindful of that when purchasing materials.

Bristol Board – This board comes in a variety of plies (1, 2, 3, 4, and so on) and may be used instead of binder's board for a thinner, more flexible, cover. It has a similar feel and appearance to office file folders.

Museum Board – This board is completely archival and is used in museums and galleries to mat artwork. Museum board may be used instead of binder's board for covers and boxes and is much easier to cut. However, the board dents easily compared to bristol or binder's board. It is generally white in appearance.

OTHER MATERIALS

Book Cloth – This is typically made with a natural or organic material such as cotton, linen, or silk. Many book cloths are backed with paper or a thin layer of paste or sizing as with library cloth. A barrier is necessary so that the adhesive does not seep through the weave of the fabric. Book cloth may be found at most major art supply or bookbinding specialty stores. Backing fabric on your own is also an option, but it requires some practice.

Leather – Leather is perhaps the best and most forgiving material to use in bookbinding. It stretches and may be dyed easily with permanent pigments. The surface is also extremely durable compared to paper or book cloth, but it takes a great deal of practice to gain control over the material. Leather has to be pared or shaved to minimize the thickness for turning over edges (see Turning Over the Edges, page 36). The leather is used in the same manner as paper and book cloth.

DETERMINING THE GRAIN

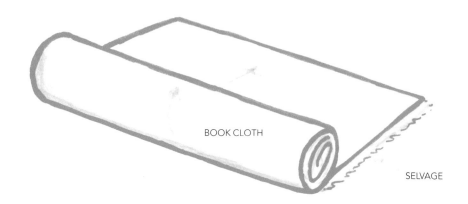

BOOK CLOTH

SELVAGE

ANOTHER IMPORTANT CONSID-eration in book and box making is the grain. The grain of a tree runs up and down, perpendicular to the ground. The same holds true when constructing a book: the grain should be parallel to the spine to give it strength and continuity. The materials fold, cut, and tear easiest along the grain.

Most bookbinding materials have a grain. Since the majority of these materials are machine milled, the grain is consistent with each product. The grain is determined by the direction in which the paper fibers are aligned or pulled. Handmade paper is pulled with a screen straight up from a vat of pulp suspended in water, rather than run along in one continuous direction. So, handmade paper does not have a discernable grain.

Check all of the materials before cutting or gluing for the proper grain direction. For book cloth, the grain is typically parallel to the selvage, or outer edge, of the cloth. This is counterintuitive, because when purchasing the cloth it is typically rolled cross-grain and cut by the yard or meter. Opposing grain directions when gluing causes irregular warping and is a big no-no in book and box making. Below are four different methods for testing the grain direction.

TIP Even computer and copy paper have a grain and should be checked before construction. Using tabloid (11 " × 17 " [27.9 × 43.2 cm]) size paper is often easier and gives more options when folding, compared to the letter sheet size of 8½" × 11" (21.6 × 27.9 cm).

Testing the Grain Direction

METHOD I ▼

The most effective and least damaging way to check the paper, board, and cloth grain is to slightly bend or roll over the material. With a consistent amount of pressure, bounce the material in one direction on a flat surface. Then turn the material 90 degrees. Roll it over and bounce with the same amount of pressure in the new direction. The direction that has the most give is the direction of the grain. Picture that the material is being wrapped around a tree trunk, where the grain is parallel to the tree.

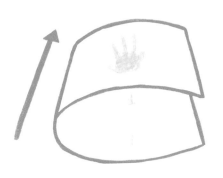

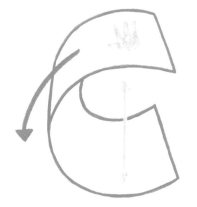

METHOD II ▶

Pinching the paper or cloth roughly along the two adjacent edges causes a heavier ripple in the direction of the grain, but damages the surface. This method does not work for the binder's board.

METHOD III ▶

Another way to check the grain is to wet the material with a spray bottle and see which way the material naturally bows or curls. If this method is chosen the material should be dried and flattened before gluing or folding. Be warned, this may permanently damage some materials.

METHOD IV ▶

If the grain is still difficult to discern, many papers have a watermark or embossment on the paper surface. When held up to a light, the sheet reveals a slightly transparent name or paper company logo. The grain runs parallel to this watermark. Most artists and writers avoid the watermark because it may become more prominent when printing or using surface treatments.

CUTTING TECHNIQUES

CUTTING DOWN THE MATERIALS is important and requires precision for some constructions. The adage holds true, "Measure twice, cut once." The materials may be either cut or torn down to size. Personal preference and aesthetics are important to the final look of the book. Torn edges have a natural and handcrafted feel, whereas a cut edge reveals a cleaner, more professional appearance. Try both!

Squaring the Materials

Many of the large sheets of paper and board have a deckled or rough edge when purchased. This is created during fabrication. These uneven edges make aligning and folding less accurate. When the material needs to be cut, it is important to have a sharp blade to achieve the cleanest edge possible. Any time the material snags or looks chewed along the edge, the blade is dull and should be replaced.

1 ▼ To square off the material, cut a clean line on the longest edge about ¼" (6 mm) from the edge.

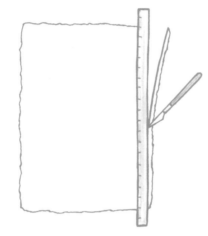

2 ▼ Turn the material 90 degrees and place the ruler along the cut edge. Then place the triangle flush to the edge of the ruler to ensure a right angle. Carefully cut along the edge and trim about ¼" (6 mm) from the edge.

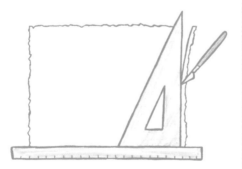

3 Use this 90-degree corner as a basis for all other measurements to ensure square edges.

Board should be squared up in the same manner as paper or cloth. Marking the board with pencil lines for the grain direction is helpful, because the grain may be more difficult to determine when the board is cut into smaller pieces.

Squaring the materials is different from the *square* of a book. The square is the extra space around the edges of the cover. It is important to mention that most books and boxes have a square. The covering material is intentionally larger to protect the pages or inside material. The number of edges with a square depends on the structure. Boxes typically have four squares where books typically have three. A standard measurement for the square is ¹⁄₁₆" or ⅛" (2 or 3 mm). (see Bookbinding Terms, page 12).

TIP When cutting materials that require the same height, mark and cut the height first to ensure that all pieces are the same. Then cut the width for each piece as needed. This is especially helpful with the boards and generally minimizes waste.

Creating Torn and Deckled Edges

Paper is typically torn with the face side down. Doing so pulls the paper fibers back to create a softer, more natural look. To discern the face side of a piece of paper, take a close look to see if there is a faint grid pattern. This is typically the back side of the paper, because as it is produced, the paper pulp lies on top of a screen as the water is extruded. The face side often has a more textured surface; some papers, however, have a smooth finish on both sides, making it difficult to determine the front from the back. A watermark can also aid in determining the correct side (see Determining the Grain—Method IV, page 19).

Torn edges may be created to mimic the natural deckled edge of the material. Tearing less than ¼" (6 mm) is challenging; 1" (2.5 cm) or more is recommended for easier tearing. For heavier papers, fold the paper in both directions to stress the fold before tearing. Here are three methods for tearing paper.

METHOD I

1 Carefully mark where the paper is to be torn with a pencil or by punching a small hole with a pin tool.

2 ▼ Line up a straight edge or ruler with the marks and place one hand on the ruler to stabilize the material.

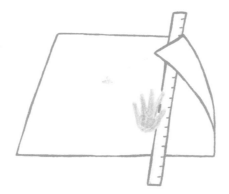

3 Use the other hand to pull the paper toward the opposite shoulder. Walk the stabilizing hand down the ruler as the paper is being torn to prevent any slipping. Tearing in short bursts gives better control and a more consistent edge.

METHOD II

1 Fold the paper in half (see Folding Techniques, page 23), then use the bone folder or butter knife to tear open the edge.

2 Keep the bone folder almost parallel to the gutter of the paper, tearing the paper slowly toward the opposite shoulder. This ensures a cleaner edge, because the more perpendicular the bone folder is to the gutter of the fold, the larger and more unpredictable the tearing. This takes a little practice and some papers tear better than others.

3 ▼ Work across the folded edge all the way to the end until the sheet is released. A nonserrated butter knife or letter opener is a great tool to decrease the chance of having too rough an edge.

(continued)

Trimming the Text Block

(continued from page 21)

METHOD III

1 ▼ Fold a sheet of paper in half. Use a small clean paintbrush with water to dampen the folded edge.

2 Allow the water to soak into the paper and tear, pulling the two sides away from one another. A straight edge may be used in conjunction with this method if desired. This makes a softer more pronounced torn edge, especially with thinner papers.

Trimming the text block is preferred for some structures to eliminate uneven edges. Typically the foredge is trimmed with single signature bindings, because of the inevitable stair stepping (see Pamphlet Stitch with Wraparound Cover and Tab, page 42).

1 Measure the text block from the spine edge and mark where it is to be trimmed. It is advisable to have at least ⅛" (3 mm) or more for trimming, because a smaller amount tends to shred the edges.

2 Line the ruler or triangle with the marks. A weight may be used to secure the ruler so that it does not slip while cutting.

3 ▼ The blade should be positioned straight up and down to ensure that the foredge is square to the table surface. Begin cutting and let the pages release slowly. The biggest mistake made is to try to cut through the entire text block all at once. Each pass with the craft knife should take off one or two pages. Having a fresh blade speeds up the process and yields a much cleaner edge. Continue until all of the pages are released.

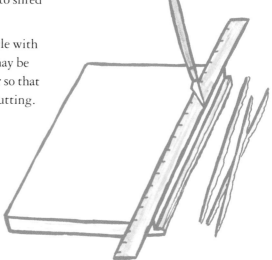

FOLDING TECHNIQUES

Scoring the Paper

FOLDING PAPER IS ESSENTIAL in book and box construction. Knowing that paper folds best when going with the grain alleviates many problems. Everyone has folded a sheet of paper and swore that it was lined up properly, yet it still revealed a misaligned edge. The following method ensures a clean folded edge every time and decreases the chance of slipping.

1   Line up the loose ends of the paper.

2   Use one hand to stabilize the
▼   positioned paper and the other hand to pinch the center of the intended folded edge.

3   With one hand still stabilizing
▼   the paper, use the bone folder on the beveled (sharper) edge to fold from the center out in both directions. Holding the paper minimizes the chance of any slipping.

TIP When bone folders are purchased they have a fatter edge than a butter knife or letter opener. The edges of the bone folder may be sanded for a sharper edge. This makes scoring and tearing more exact. To compensate for a fatter scoring tool, move the ruler or triangle slightly away from the measured line and then score.

Scoring the paper makes folding a snap. Most papers benefit from scoring before folding to yield a cleaner edge. Heavy papers are often difficult to fold even when going with the grain. Scoring compresses the fibers, guiding the paper to a nice folded edge. Folding against the grain is sometimes necessary and this typically prevents a cracked edge.

1   Mark the intended scored edge and align the ruler or triangle with the marks. *Note:* If a 90-degree angle is desired, a ruler should be lined up with one edge of the material first. Then a triangle may be placed along the edge of a ruler.

2   Use one hand to stabilize the
▼   ruler. Then use the tip of the bone folder or butter knife to make a clean line along the edge. The amount of pressure and number of passes varies on the thickness of the material.

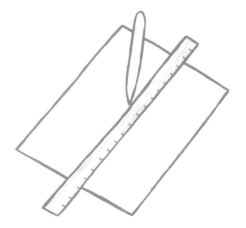

Orientation and Signatures

Books purchased from an antique or used bookstore may reveal a sealed edge. The sealed pages are a result of the layout or folding of the pages before binding. As a bonus, the reader knew that he or she was the first to read that book. Roughly every four to eight pages would be sealed at the head and/or foredge. Historically, having books made required money, making it less available to the lower income families. Today, paper and other materials are reproduced cheaply, giving access to almost everyone. Recycled materials are a great resource for constructing a book or box and require little to no money.

A gathering of pages creates what is commonly referred to as a *signature.* Multiple signatures are used to build the thickness or height of a book, sewing one signature on top of the next.

The orientation for a folded sheet of paper is dependent upon the grain. Most paper grain runs either vertically or horizontally with the length as the paper is positioned up and down. As a general rule, when a piece of paper is folded in half with the grain, this determines the final shape of the folded signature. Nested folios may also be used to create a signature

(see Pamphlet Stitch with Wrap-around Cover and Tab, page 42). For example, if folios are used and a square text block is desired, measure the height and cut the paper. Then take that measurement and double for the width. The sheet, when folded, makes a perfect square shape.

Paper is typically not folded more than three times for a signature, because the alignment of the paper decreases, and punching sewing stations becomes increasingly difficult. Relieving the pressure is important when folding a single piece of paper more than once, because the paper may kink or wrinkle along the gutter of the

signature. This effect increases when using heavier papers. The following two methods create a *self-contained* signature requiring no clips.

QUARTO

To make a quarto, the paper is folded twice. The first fold is against the grain and the second is with the grain (see Determining the Grain, page 18). The final size of the signature is one-quarter of the original size.

1 Make the first fold, then tear a little more than halfway down the folded edge (see Creating Torn and Deckled Edges—Method II, page 21).

2 Grab the loose ends tightly and
▼ line up the edge to make the second and final fold.

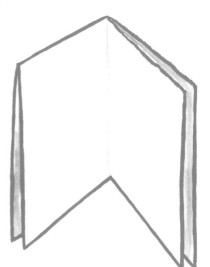

OCTAVO

To make an octavo, the paper is folded three times. The first fold is with the grain, the second is against the grain, and the third is with the grain (see Determining the Grain, page 18). The final size of the signature is one-eighth of the original size.

1 Make the first fold, then tear a
▼ little more than halfway down the folded edge (see Creating Torn and Deckled Edges—Method II, page 21).

2 Grab the loose ends tightly and
▼ line up to make the second fold. Tear a little more than halfway again to relieve the pressure. The second tearing goes through two sheets at once. Depending on the paper stock chosen, this may take more effort.

3 Pinch the loose ends and fold
▼ a third time to complete the signature.

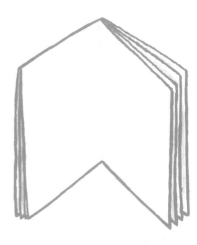

SEWING TECHNIQUES

NOT ALL BOOKS HAVE TO BE sewn, but many are. This section explains how to create holes or sewing stations for sewing, use a jig for multiple signatures, decide which thread to use, and secure and join threads.

Punching Sewing Stations

Sewing stations, or holes, are created so that the needle and thread may pass through more easily. There are different ways of handling this task; most artists, however, rely on a flat surface and a pin tool or awl. A punching cradle is a helpful tool to use and is easy to make. It drastically speeds up the punching process and is great to have around when making multiples. When sewing stations are needed along the spine, it is best to use a punching board made from several pieces of scrap binder's board or a block of wood so the table surface does not become damaged.

TIP A simple version of a punching cradle can be made out of binder's board and may be constructed with PVA and/or heavy packing tape, but it does not last as long.

PUNCHING BY HAND

1 Make pencil marks along the gutter of the signature as desired. Lay the book flat on the table. Line up the pin tool or awl with one of the pencil marks and close the book.

2 ▼ Push directly out, keeping the pin tool parallel to the table surface. When using the awl, consider the thickness of the post so as not to punch too large of a sewing station. Repeat for any other marks.

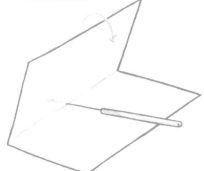

MAKING A PUNCHING CRADLE

1 ▼ Take two long boards (24" × 4" [61 × 10.2 cm]) and lay one along the edge of the other. Drill holes along the edge and screw the boards together so they form a 90-degree angle.

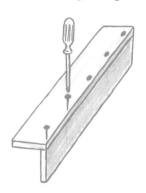

2 ▼ Place the corner edge down like like a V, and screw to it a piece of wood measuring 4" × 8" (10.2 × 20.3 cm) to stabilize the end. This gives a solid base from which to work. If desired, another piece of wood may be added to the other end for greater stability.

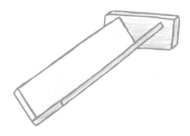

3 ▼ To punch the sewing stations, lay the signature so that the peak falls neatly into the cradle. Use a pin tool or awl to punch straight down. Having the boards flush together stops the punching tool from penetrating the signature too deeply.

Multiple Signatures and Creating a Jig

For books that have multiple signatures, create a template, or jig, to ensure that all of the holes line up neatly for each signature. This is especially important for exposed bindings where the stitching shows along the spine edge. The jig also saves from having to measure each signature individually. *Note:* A spring divider is a great tool to use for making multiple marks that require the same distance.

1   Cut a scrap piece of heavy paper about 1" (2.5 cm) wide and the exact height of the signature. Old file folders work well for a jig and can be reused for future projects.

2   Make marks along one edge of the jig for the appropriate sewing stations.

3   Paper-clip the jig to the signature so that the marks line up with the gutter of the signature. Punch the sewing stations for each mark. Replace the jig for each signature and punch in the same manner. *Note:* Plastic-coated paper clips work best because they do not mark up the surface of the materials

Thread and Sewing Materials

Many different threads and materials may be used to sew books together. Linen thread, leather cording, and plastic lanyards are just a few of the items that have made their way into artist's books. Whatever is used to sew the text block together, the sewing stations need to be large enough to accommodate the thickness of the thread. As a note, thicker sewing materials may make the inside pages bulge and cause indentations. Below is a listing of some bookbinding threads and alternative materials.

LINEN THREAD: The thread is great to use because of its strength and archival properties. It comes in a variety of colors and thicknesses. Natural-colored linen thread holds up to dyeing, so the possibilities are endless. Each company has its own way of measuring the thickness of the threads, but typically thread can be judged by how many strings, or plies, are twisted together (1, 2, 3, 4, etc). Linen thread is much stronger than embroidery thread and is used most frequently in bookbinding (see page 14).

WAXED LINEN THREAD: Waxed linen thread is the same as regular linen thread, except that it has a coating of beeswax. Plain linen thread may be passed through a piece of beeswax instead of buying a separate spool of waxed thread. This is often preferable because many waxed linen threads have too thick of a coating. Waxed thread is ideal for exposed bindings because the layer of wax seals the thread. To remove any excess wax, scrape the thread between two fingernails.

SILK THREAD: This is a beautiful thread to use for more delicate bindings. The texture of the thread is smooth and glides easily through the sewing stations. A wide variety of colors are available.

EMBROIDERY THREAD: This cotton thread comes in a wide range of colors and has a very soft texture. Because of the multiple strings that make up the thread, it may be easily separated to the desired thickness. Securing the thread is not an option when using embroidery thread, because the threads are not twisted tightly together like the linen thread.

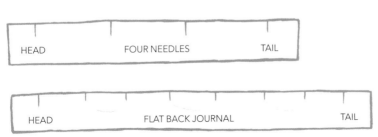

HEAD   FOUR NEEDLES   TAIL

HEAD   FLAT BACK JOURNAL   TAIL

Securing the Thread

LEATHER CORDING: Leather is fantastic to use and extremely strong but requires much larger sewing stations. It adds a considerable amount of bulk to the text block and does not work well in conjunction with thin papers.

METAL WIRE: Metal wire is an interesting alternative for sewing. Colored wire may be found in most art supply and craft stores in a wide variety of thicknesses and finishes. A needle is not required with most wires, but a pair of pliers is helpful to ensure the stitching stays tight. Wire works best with heavier papers and/or board, to avoid tearing or ripping the materials.

TIP When sewing, the desired amount of tightness is often referred to as bookbinder's tension. Some constructions do not require tight sewing, because the spine may be reinforced later. Conversely, stitching that is too tight may not allow the text block to close properly. Somewhere in between is desirable.

Securing the thread is one of the handiest tricks when sewing and decreases bulk when compared to doubling the thread. And the most important reason for securing the thread is that the needle does not fall off while sewing. Remember to choose a needle that is roughly the same thickness as the thread being used.

I Use the blunt end of the bone
▼ folder to flatten the end of the thread. Grab the thread close to the end and thread through the eye of the needle. Leave a short tail of about 4" to 5" (10.2 to 12.7 cm).

2 Pierce the needle through the
▼ short tail 2" (5.1 cm) from the edge.

3 Keep the needle straight up and
▼ down, pointed side up. Pull the short tail all the way down past the eye of the needle.

4 Continue to hold the needle straight up and down. Pull on the long thread perpendicular to the needle until the slipknot meets the eye of the needle. Be careful not to pull too hard. If the short tail is pierced too close to the edge, the excessive pressure could unravel the shorter tail and fall off.

5 The thread is now secured to the needle. After sewing is complete, snip off any remaining thread.

Weaver's Knot (Joining Thread Together)

Once in a while, the thread runs out or becomes damaged. Learning to join a new thread is not always a favorite task among new bookbinders, but it is necessary when creating thick text blocks with many signatures. The old and new thread may be joined easily by following the steps below.

1 Make sure that there is enough thread to join; 4" to 6" (10.2 to 15.2 cm) is sufficient. The thread is typically joined on the inside of a signature, but may be joined along the spine as well. Back up the thread if necessary to the appropriate side.

2 ▼ Loop the thread as if tying a knot. Instead of pulling the end of the thread through to complete the knot, leave a small loop.

3 ▼ Hold on to the two ends and pull the loop through slightly to make a slipknot.

4 ▼ Position the knot close to the sewing station. Then slip the new thread through the loop of the old thread.

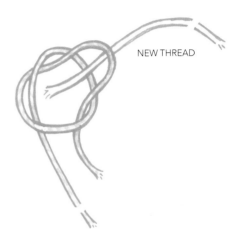

NEW THREAD

5 ▼ Pull tightly on both strings on the old thread to secure. Trim down any excess thread to ¼" (6 mm).

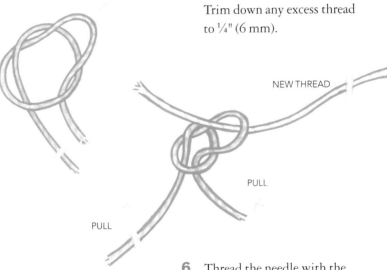

NEW THREAD

PULL

PULL

6 Thread the needle with the new thread and secure to continue sewing.

ADHESIVES

THE ABUNDANCE OF GLUES AND adhesives available on the market can be overwhelming. This section presents an explanation of adhesives and their proper uses. As a book artist, it is important to consider the archival property of each adhesive. It is also important to know how an adhesive adheres and how it spreads across the surface. Evaluate gluing by investigating the quality and strength of each product. Paying attention to the properties of the adhesives and materials will give the book longevity.

The adhesives commonly available have either a synthetic or organic base. The two adhesives used by artists are polyvinyl acetate (PVA) and methyl cellulose, because they are readily available and consistently acid free. Check the product container for archival properties or contact the company before use (see Archival Materials, page 16).

How an adhesive reacts to the materials is important. The tack or how sticky the adhesive is gives an indication of how quickly it dries. The heavier or tackier the glue, the faster it will dry. An even spread, or glide, of the adhesive with no breaks in the brushstrokes across the surface is ideal. This also allows for a faster application of the adhesive. With some projects, a lighter mixture may be ideal to increase the open time of the adhesive, allowing the artist to move, replace, or reposition the elements before they are completely secured to the surface. Also, it is important to note that papers stretch more across the grain and thinner papers tend to stretch the most.

If the book becomes damaged or in need of repair, it is important to know if the adhesive is reversible, as with book restoration. This makes the replacement of various parts much easier. Knowing what mixtures to use and how they affect the material comes with experience. Remember to always test the materials before working on any project.

Real *glue* is derived from animal products. This requires a regulated heat source, and is typically not used in contemporary bookbinding because of the special setup required. Most people continue to use the word *glue* when referring to adhesives. For clarity, all glues will be referred to as an adhesive, paste or PVA. What follows are some of the adhesives available.

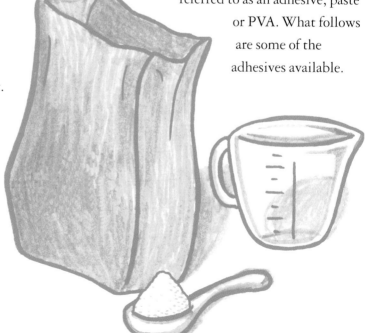

PASTES

Cooked pastes have a vegetable/grain base and require a relatively longer drying time. Most paste recipes are a mixture of water and flour or starch, which require cooking. Flours can be made up of wheat, rice, or cornstarch. Methyl cellulose, the synthetic counterpart, is a commonly used paste among artists because it lasts one to two months compared to cooked pastes, which last only two to four days.

The term *shelf life* refers to the life of an adhesive kept at room temperature. To prolong a cooked paste's shelf life, use purified water or keep it refrigerated up to several weeks. To use the paste later, it should be reheated and may require a small amount of water to loosen the mixture. The only downside to using methyl cellulose instead of a cooked paste is that the bond is not quite as strong. To compensate for this problem when using a mixture of adhesives, use a two-thirds PVA to one-third methyl cellulose ratio instead of a one-half PVA to one-half paste ratio.

SYNTHETIC ADHESIVES

Synthetic adhesives are human-made and similar in appearance to most common white glues, such as school glue. PVA is a premixed, heavier adhesive with a shorter drying time. PVA can be thinned down with water; it is recommended, however, to thin down the PVA with a lighter weight paste instead. The water, if used too much, may weaken the bond of the glue. Jade paste is a common form of PVA that may be found in most art supply stores. School glue is a form of PVA, but is brittle by comparison. The flexibility of the PVA is preferable. PVA lasts a year or longer if it does not become contaminated with another paste or impure water.

GLUE STICKS

Most glue stick manufacturers have incorporated an archival adhesive stick that has a decent semipermanent to permanent bond. A glue stick is primarily used for simple constructions or models and should not be relied on for more substantial projects. It works best when adhering lightweight papers to another porous surface.

DOUBLE-SIDED TAPE

Double-sided tape works very well, almost too well. Select a tape that is archival; this may be used in place of thin applications of adhesive, as with tipping on paper (see Tipping On and Hinging Panels, page 35). The tape is available in a variety of widths. A large adhesive sheet may also be purchased, but is often not as cost effective and leaves little room for error. Both the tape and sheet create a permanent bond, but are unforgiving if the structure needs to be taken apart. Keep in mind, once the item is placed down, it does not move!

RUBBER CEMENT

Never use rubber cement. Some artists are enticed by its easy control and quick bond. However, rubber cement is not archival, and falls apart in approximately two to twelve months after construction. Do not use any adhesive that has a lacquer or acetone base. Synthetic adhesives of this nature are typically cold to the touch, barring any products that contain mint or clove oil. The chemicals in rubber cement absorb quickly into the skin. With long-term exposure, allergies and/or damage to the central nervous system may arise, causing irritation or numbness to the extremities. This is very bad stuff!

Mixing Adhesives and Recommended Uses

Mixing adhesives is like cooking; find the best mixtures by testing the materials to see how they react. Below are some standard mixtures and recommended uses. The drying time of each adhesive is dependent on how much paste is used in relation to the environmental conditions. Adhesives dry more quickly in a warm, dry environment, whereas a cool and humid work space could double the drying time. The complete drying time for most adhesives is at least an hour, but it is preferable to allow projects to dry overnight. The project is dry when it is no longer damp or cool to the touch.

PASTE 100 PERCENT
slow drying time

- paper to paper
- thin natural fibers
- papier mâché
- backing fabric
- leather to board

PASTE FIFTY PERCENT, PVA FIFTY PERCENT
medium drying time

- paper to paper
- paper to board
- book cloth to board
- natural fibers to paper
- text weight papers

PVA 100 PERCENT
quick drying time

- board to board
- heavy book cloth to board
- heavy weight papers
- wood to paper or board
- synthetic materials and papers

A good rule of thumb when using adhesives that have been out for several days is to smell them before applying to the project. If the adhesive smells sour, throw it away. Fermentation occurs when the natural yeast in the grain is allowed to cultivate and grow. Besides odor, the spoiled paste may also take on a different color—yellowish to light brown. Even synthetic adhesives may spoil if they come into contact with a contaminated water source or are mixed with a cooked paste. To prevent PVA from going bad, some companies add mint oil to the recipe.

No-Cook Adhesive Recipes

For no-cook methods, the paste should have a thick "sugar glaze" or thin "pudding" consistency. If the paste is too thin, there is an increase in drying time, making it difficult to use. The reason for this is that it oversaturates the glued material. Mix enough paste for the project in mind. The recipes below will yield a little more than 1 cup (236.6 ml) of paste. Adjust the proportions for smaller or larger projects as needed.

METHYL CELLULOSE

1 tablespoon (15–18 g) methyl cellulose

1 cup (236.6 ml) warm water (distilled)

1 Mix the ingredients in a blender or whisk until smooth.

2 Let the mixture stand for at least one hour after mixing for best results. The mixture expands and thickens as it sets. Add small amounts of methyl cellulose powder or water to achieve the desired consistency.

Result when dry: smooth paste

Color: clear colorless gel

Cooked Adhesive Recipes

WALLPAPER PASTE

4 to 5 tablespoons (40 to 50 g)
  wallpaper paste

1¼ cup (295.7 ml) warm water
  (distilled)

1 Mix the ingredients in blender
or whisk until smooth.

2 For a less grainy paste, cook in
a pan to a slow boil, stirring
constantly. Turn down the heat
and continue stirring for three
to five minutes. *Note:* Some
wallpaper pastes in powder form
contain a poison to deter bugs
and rodents. Read all labels
before using. Keep out of reach
of children and pets.

Result when dry: grainy paste

Color: slight ivory cast

TIP Remember to always
keep the adhesives covered
when not in use. This prevents a skin from forming
on the surface. Plastic containers with a lid are ideal for
storing unused adhesives.
Placing a board or a sheet
of wax paper over the glue
pot between applications
is also an effective way of
reducing the air contact.

1 Mix the starch with lukewarm
water until it is completely
dissolved.

2 Cook in a saucepan or double
boiler and bring to a boil.

3 Reduce the heat and stir
constantly for three to five
minutes. The paste thickens as
it cools.

WHEAT STARCH

3½ tablespoons* (30.8 g) wheat starch
  *1 tablespoon = 8.8 g

2 cups (473.2 ml) water

Result when dry: smooth
paste/minor embossed paper

Color: watery skim milk

CORNSTARCH

3 tablespoons* (30 g) cornstarch
  *1 tablespoon = 10 g

3 cups (709.8 ml) water

Result when dry: smooth paste/
softly embossed paper

Color: watery skim milk

TAPIOCA STARCH

4 tablespoons* (34 g) tapioca starch
  *1 tablespoon = 8.5 g

3 cups (709.8 ml) water

Result when dry: smooth paste/
minimally dimpled paper

Color: watery skim milk

POTATO STARCH

3 tablespoons* (34.5 g) potato starch
  *1 tablespoon = 11.5 g

3 cups (709.8 ml) water

Result when dry: smooth paste/
minimally dimpled paper

Color: watery skim milk

MOCHIKO—SWEET RICE FLOUR STARCH

4 tablespoons* (42 g) mochiko
  *1 tablespoon = 10.5 g

3 cups (709.8 ml) water

Result when dry: smooth paste/
softly embossed paper

Color: watery skim milk

WHEAT FLOUR

7 tablespoons* (63 g) wheat flour
  *1 tablespoon = 9 g

3 cups (709.8 ml) water

Result when dry: smooth paste/
highly embossed paper

Color: yellowish ivory

Gluing Techniques

Gluing Board

SCRAP AND WAXED PAPER ARE helpful companions when gluing. Prepare the proper mixture of adhesive for the project (see Adhesives, page 30). Remember to test all the materials before construction to alleviate any problems with the final project. *Any time an adhesive is used, place the project under weight until it is completely dry.* This is discussed in detail further along in this section.

Always mix enough adhesive for the entire project. This ensures consistency in the application and how the materials react to being glued. When gluing one material to another, glue the smaller of the two surfaces for less mess and better control. In general, applying an adhesive works best from the center out in all directions. This decreases the chance of getting the adhesive on any unintended areas. It is not an exact science, but each material reacts differently by stretching, becoming more delicate as with tissue papers, wrinkling, and curling.

Synthetic adhesives such as PVA can easily stain the paper and book cloth. Mistakes happen even to the most experienced bookbinder. Make a habit of folding over any used scrap paper and get it away from the project. In the event that an adhesive makes its way onto the project, allow it to dry completely before removing. Smearing the adhesive only pushes it deeper into the material. Use the rubber cement pick-up eraser to remove any dried adhesive. This eraser picks up PVA the best, but make sure it is completely dry before erasing. The white plastic eraser may also be used to remove light stains from gluing. The following methods describe different ways of applying adhesives.

1 ▼ Glue the board from the center out in all directions, and place on the back side of the paper or cloth.

2 Smooth the back side of the board to ensure it is sticking to the covering material.

3 Flip over the board and smooth out the face side to get rid of any wrinkles or air bubbles. The bone folder may be used on the flat edge to smooth the materials. Use a piece of clean paper under the bone folder to avoid marking up the paper or cloth.

Tipping On and Hinging Panels

Tipping on is the method of joining several sheets of paper together by using a thin line of adhesive. Gluing a ⅛" (3 mm) strip of adhesive is a standard amount for tipping on a piece of paper. A larger measurement gives more stability, but may decrease the flexibility of the paper. Additional reinforcement may be needed depending on the project.

1 Measure and mark the area to be tipped on. Lay down a piece of scrap paper larger than the item being glued and place the material on top.

2 Use a clean strip of scrap paper with a straight edge and align it to the marked edge. This functions as a mask while gluing.

3 ▼ Carefully apply the adhesive along the tipped edge, brushing from the masked edge onto the paper. Remove the mask and scrap paper from underneath the project. It is best to use as little adhesive as possible so that it does not spill over the edges.

4 Place the new material directly to the glued surface and use the bone folder to smooth.

HINGING PANELS

Hinging panels may be required when making larger book formats, especially with accordions (see Accordion with Woven Panels, page 54). A tab is created to join two sheets together or to lengthen a text block. The tab is typically no smaller than ¼" (6 mm). For greater stability, use ½" (1.3 cm). Hinging is normally done on the back side of the text block to hide the tab. Use the adhesive most appropriate for the materials being used. The following two methods are most commonly used.

ATTACHED TAB

1 ▼ Fold the tab over first before any additional folding. For accordion panels it is important to cut the paper the same size and create a tab for both pieces. Even though only one tab may actually be used, this ensures an exact fit when the text block is closed.

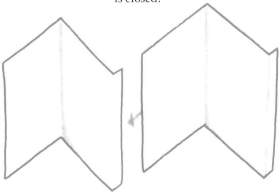

2 Use the previous method of tipping on to glue the two sheets together. Repeat if necessary.

Turning Over the Edges

Corner Options

TISSUE PAPER

A single piece of paper may also be used to join two sheets together, but may create a slight gap between the two sheets when folding. A thin Japanese tissue paper works best because it does not add as much bulk to the page. A torn edge for the hinging paper blends the papers together in comparison to a cut edge (see Creating Torn and Deckled Edges, page 21).

1 Lay the two sheets facedown and
▼ align the edges to be hinged. Then glue the hinging paper.

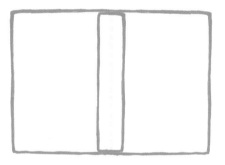

2 Carefully place the hinging paper to the back side of the two sheets so there is an even amount on both sheets. Smooth out and allow to lie flat until completely dry before folding. Repeat if necessary.

A turn-in covers the edges of the board and creates an overlap so that the board does not show. A standard turn-in is ⅝" (1.6 cm). When the paper or cloth is turned over the board, it gives an even ½" (1.3 cm) edge. It is more difficult to turn-in any edges smaller than ½" (1.3 cm). Often an end sheet is glued to cover a majority of a turn-in; the overlap, however, ensures a neater look and a more stable structure.

To assist in preparing the turn-ins for any project, a cheater's strip may be cut from any scrap board to a thickness of ⅝" (1.6 cm) and a length of 12" (30.5 cm) or longer (see Tools, page 13). This is used in a number of ways throughout the book. A metal strip may be purchased at a hardware store for a more durable tool to cut against. The spring divider may be used instead to score the distance along each edge.

Corners need to be cut before gluing the turn-ins to minimize bulk and to create a cleaner edge. Corners may be handled in one of three ways, each having a distinctive look. Measure at least one board thickness away from the corner to avoid exposing the board once the edges are turned in. The thickness of the cheater's strip may be used as a guide if it is the same thickness as the covered board.

TIP The use of triangles creates exact corners. To assist in preparation, mark each appropriate angle on the triangle with a permanent marker for easy reference (see Triangular Box, page 100). Experienced binders do quite a bit of eyeballing with corners and simple measurements that are eventually covered. Comfort comes with experience.

MITERED CORNER ▶

A 45/45/90-degree triangle is helpful for this corner option (see page 14). Mark a 45-degree angle a board thickness away on both sides of the corner and cut. After both edges are turned over, it creates a nice mitered corner, just like a picture frame.

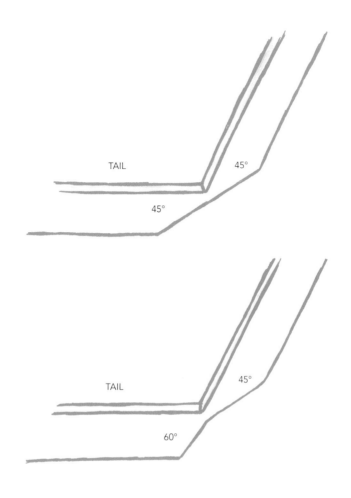

OVERLAPPING CORNER ▶

Both 45/45/90- and 30/60/90-degree triangles are needed for this corner. Mark a 60-degree angle at the head and tail, a board thickness away from the corner. Then mark a 45-angle at the foredge of the board, also a board thickness away. This option has a stronger overlap than the mitered corner and is seen on many commercial bindings to ensure a covered corner.

LIBRARY CORNER ▶

Do not cut the corner for this option. Glue the corner of the covering material and wrap it over the board to create a neat square. Pinch the edges where the paper meets up with the edges of the board to ensure that it is snug against the thickness of the board. Repeat for any other corners before gluing the side turn-ins. *Note:* This creates a bulkier corner and is not ideal with thicker covering materials.

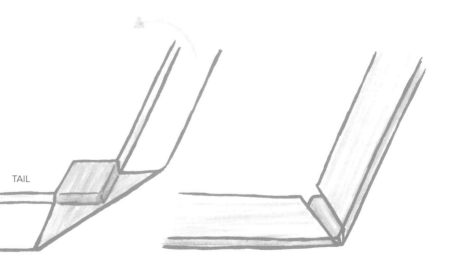

GLUING THE TURN-INS AND CORNERS

1 Use a cheater's strip to measure ⅝" (1.6 cm) around all of the edges of the glued board and cut. Choose the desired corner option for finishing off the edge.

2 ▼ Glue one turn-in and place the project at the edge of the table. Use your pointer finger and thumb in an L shape to press from the center out in both directions along the thickness of the board. Then turn-in the overlap to the back side of the board and press into place. Pinch the slight overhang on both ends straight down to avoid pointed corners.

3 ▼ Use the bone folder on the turn-in to ensure a good bond. Repeat the procedure above for any remaining turn-ins. For consistency, turn-in the opposite side, then proceed to any adjacent sides.

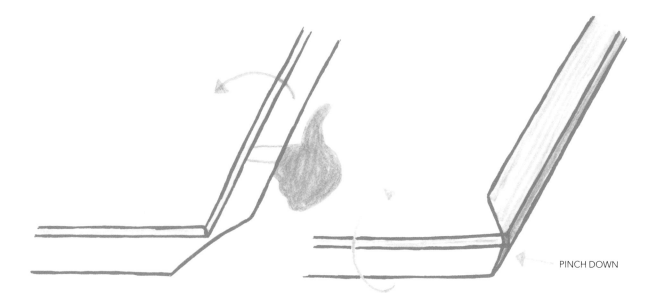

PINCH DOWN

Keeping the Projects Flat

Any time that an adhesive or moisture is applied to a project, it has a tendency to warp or buckle. Boards and weights are used to press the book or box to ensure a tight bond, free of wrinkles and unsightly warping.

BOOK PRESS (shown below): A book press is ideal because it exerts an even amount of pressure over the project. They tend to be expensive and difficult to find in some areas. This professional piece of equipment, however, is a great investment. Make sure the book press rests on a sturdy surface that is able to handle the weight.

BOARDS: Wooden boards are easy to acquire and when sealed with polyurethane work extremely well. Make sure the boards are completely flat and have a smooth finish. Any curves or bowing in the boards will transfer to the project.

CLAMPS: Any clamps may be used when pressing a project. Some clamps have a trigger grip to apply the pressure and may come with protective rubber ends. These tend to work better than traditional C-clamps, because they do not create indentations on the material surface.

Essentially any flat object larger than the project may be used for pressing. The same is true for the weight. A brick wrapped in a freezer bag or cloth is just as useful as a stack of encyclopedias. The more pressure that can be applied, the less chance of wrinkling and warping.

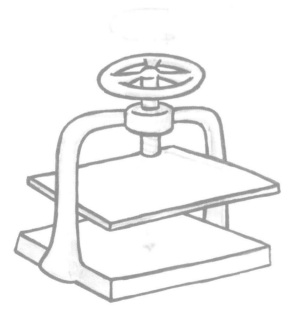

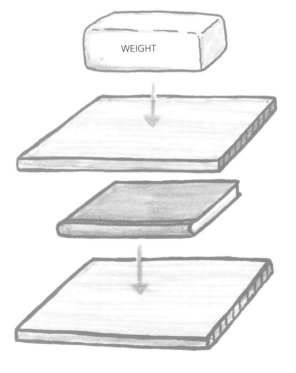

WEIGHT

2

A VARIETY OF DIFFERENT BOOK STRUC-
tures are demonstrated in this section.
Follow along and complete each
project to get a better understanding of
the basic principles in bookbinding. Each
project builds on the next. Practicing with
the materials and the projects will open
the door to experimentation. Have fun by
combining the various formats to create
a unique book. Exact measurements and a
formula are given to assist in preparation for
each project. The formulas can be used as a
guide to create customized shapes and sizes.

The eleven book projects are each distinctive in appearance and construction. The
first three books are nonadhesive structures,
which focus on the five-hole pamphlet
stitch and offer a choice of two covers: a
wraparound and a paper-wrapped board.
A book sewn with four needles and a simple
folded cover constitutes the third nonadhesive book. The unique aspect of this book
is that the exposed spine enables the book to
open completely flat. Creating each of these
books is a great way to get comfortable with
the materials before using any adhesives.

The next four projects cover variations
on the accordion. These folded books
include an eight-panel woven accordion,
a star accordion, a spiral or zig-zag
accordion, and a triangle accordion.

The next book has an exposed side stitch
that functions like a flip book. This stab
binding is a fantastic opportunity to use
single sheets. The pages are secured with
a traditional inner binding and decorative
corner tabs. The cross pattern shown is the
focus, but visual examples are given for
three additional patterns.

The next two books have a hard cover
with a reinforced spine. Headbands complete the first two books. The perfect-bound
book is created with folded sheets, adhesive,
and absolutely no sewing. The unsupported
link stitch is ideal for sketchbooks, diaries,
and photo albums, and the insets create a
beautiful accent to this more traditional
book structure. The last project demonstrates how to make a wonderful double
picture frame that folds up like a portfolio.

Have fun and try them all!

FORMULA FOR THE MATERIALS

Text Block   HEIGHT = desired book size

WIDTH = 2 × desired book size (add ¹/₂" [1.3 cm] if trimming foredge)

Cover   HEIGHT = height of text block plus ¹/₄" (6 mm) (square for head and tail)

WIDTH = 4¹/₂ to 5 × width of trimmed text block

Thread   LENGTH = 2¹/₂ to 3 × height of text block

MATERIALS

Six 6" × 9¹/₂" (15.2 × 24.1 cm) pieces light weight paper for the text block

One 6¹/₄" × 23" (15.9 × 58.4 cm) piece medium to heavy weight paper for the cover

18" (45.7 cm) length of linen thread for sewing

PAMPHLET STITCH

with Wraparound Cover and Tab

THIS IS A GOOD PROJECT TO START WITH BECAUSE IT focuses on several essential elements used in bookmaking: folding, sewing, and cutting. This easy-to-assemble project creates an interesting and unique format for a self-contained book with a tab closure. This single signature book is ideal for simple-page formats that can be created on the computer or photocopier. The stitch is similar to how magazines are put together with staples over the peak, or spine edge, of the signature, called a *saddle stitch.* A heavier cover stock works best for the cover.

Sewing the Text Block

1 Prepare the text block by making four to six folios (see Bookbinding Terms, page 12, and Folding Techniques, page 23). To avoid excessive stair stepping, use no more than six folios.

2 Gather the folios and nest them together, one inside the other, to form one signature.

3 Knock up, or jog, the signature along the folded
▼ (spine) edge and at the head, so the folios are aligned neatly. Then clip each side with a clothespin. The clips act as an extra set of hands while working on the cover. (Clothespins are recommended over heavier clips because they do not damage the materials.)

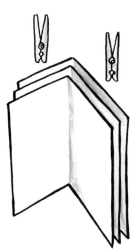

4 Lay the cover paper face up before scoring. This ensures that the nice side of the paper shows on the outside when complete. From the left edge, measure and score a line the desired width of the finished book (after the foredge is trimmed) plus ⅛" (3 mm) for the square. Fold over and crease along the scored line, to create the inside of the front cover. The paper extending on the right covers the outside and eventually becomes the flap.

TIP Stair stepping refers to the nested folios spilling out unevenly at the foredge of a text block. The amount of stair stepping greatly depends on the paper stock being used. Thinner paper or fewer folios decrease the "stair stepping" effect and are recommended for easier sewing and construction.

5 Lay the folios into the valley of the cover and give equal spacing at the head and tail. The folios hang over the foredge initially, but are trimmed down after sewing. Replace the clothespins to include the cover. The book should open freely.

6 ▼ Make a pencil mark on the inside gutter of the signature in the center. Then make two more marks ½" (1.3 cm) from the head and the tail. Find the center between each end mark and the center mark and make two additional marks. Symmetrical sewing stations create a more stable structure. There should be a total of five pencil marks.

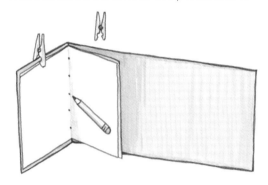

7 Lay the book flat on the table and create the sewing stations. (see Punching Sewing Stations, page 26.)

8 Thread the needle and secure (see Securing the Thread, page 28). Sew using a double figure eight as a pattern.

9 This particular stitch may be started from either the inside or outside of the book. The stitch begins and ends in the same sewing station. For this version, start on the outside of the center sewing station so the knot is hidden inside the cover after construction. Thread the needle into the center sewing station and pull through, leaving a 3" to 4" (7.6 to 10.2 cm) tail or enough to tie off at the end.

10 ▼ Exit through the next sewing station toward the head of the book. Now sew in through the sewing station nearest the head of the text block.

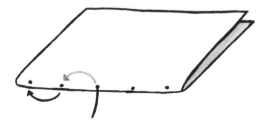

11 ▼ Go back out through the sewing station that is second from the head. Be careful not to pierce the other thread, because it makes the stitching difficult to tighten. Skip over the center sewing station and then bring the needle into the second to last sewing station from the tail.

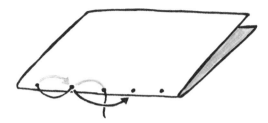

12 ▼ Exit through the last sewing station nearest the tail. Enter the second to last sewing station again and finish by exiting through the center hole.

13 ▼ Make sure there is a tail on each side of the thread of the longer stitch; this secures the longer stitch when tied. Tighten the threads by pulling in the opposite direction of the sewing. This minimizes the chance of tearing open the sewing stations. Retrace the sewing steps if the stitching does not tighten easily.

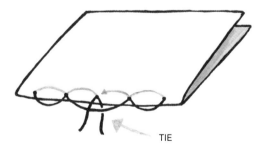

TIE

14 Tie a square knot to finish the sewing and trim off the extra thread to no smaller than ¼" (7 mm). Any shorter and the knot could come undone, making it difficult to retie.

Folding the Cover

1 Remove the clothespins, close the book and press with a bone folder along the sewn edge to flatten. Fold back the cover and measure the desired width for the text block from the sewn edge. Trim the foredge of the text block (see Trimming the Text Block, page 22) to remove any stair stepping from the nested folios. After trimming, fold the cover back to its original position.

2 ▼ Measure and score the longer cover panel to the width of the trimmed text block plus ⅛" (3 mm) for the square. Fold back the longer panel so that it wraps toward the spine.

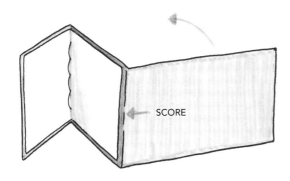

SCORE

3 ▼ A double-score is needed so the cover neatly wraps around the spine and thickness of the text block (see Scoring the Paper, page 23). Pinch the spine tightly and measure to include the thickness of the text block plus the cover. Score the first edge as it meets up with the spine, then move the triangle over and score to create a flat spine edge for the cover. The double-score for the spine should be parallel and flush against the stitched spine of the cover. Wrap the cover around to the foredge of the book.

DOUBLE- SCORE

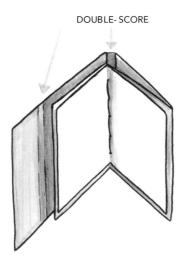

4 Measure and double-score at the foredge of the cover the width of the text block, plus the square, plus two times the cover thickness. The first score should be a little outside of where it meets up with the loose end of the cover. The second score line should compensate for the space mentioned. Then wrap it around the closed text block.

5 ▼ Create a tab on the smaller loose end, which is used as an enclosure to fasten the book closed. A tab of 1" × 1" (2.5 × 2.5 cm) or larger is recommended, because a more delicate tab does not wear well after repeated opening and closing. Fold the tab over the cover and mark a dot on each side of the tab 1" (2.5 cm) from the tip of the tab. Fold back the tab and open up the cover so it lies flat on the cutting surface. Cut a slit between the pencil marks.

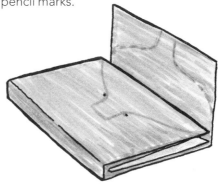

6 ▼ Fold the cover back to wrap around the text block and insert the tab into the slit.

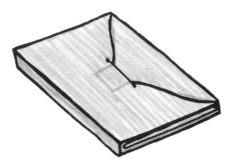

TIP By leaving the thread longer, it can be wrapped over the head and used as a page keeper. Also, if the thread is left longer for the spine edge and a wraparound cover is not used, it can be used to hang the book.

FORMULA FOR THE MATERIALS

Text Block	HEIGHT = desired book size
	WIDTH = 2 × desired book size; add ¹/₂" (1.3 cm) if trimming foredge
Binder's Board	HEIGHT = width of sewn text block
	WIDTH = width of sewn text block
Outer Cover	HEIGHT = height of board
	WIDTH = width of board plus 4" (10.2 cm)
Inner Cover	HEIGHT = height of board plus 4" (10.2 cm)
	WIDTH = width of board
Spine	HEIGHT = height of board
	WIDTH = thickness of text block plus 4" (10.2 cm)

MATERIALS

six 6" × 9¹/₂" (15.2 × 24.1 cm) pieces lightweight paper for the text block

two 6" × 4¹/₂" " (15.2 × 11.4 cm) pieces binder's board for the cover

two 6" × 8¹/₂" (15.2 × 21.6 cm) pieces medium weight paper for the outer cover

two 10" × 4¹/₂" (25.4 × 11.4 cm) pieces medium weight paper for the inner cover

one 6" × 4¹/₈" (15.2 × 10.5 cm) piece medium weight paper for the spine

18" (45.7 cm) length linen thread for sewing

Paper-Wrapped
BOARD COVER

THIS IS A POPULAR WAY OF COVERING BOOKS with several different pieces of paper wrapped over the board. Exact cutting decreases any slipping between the text block and cover. When using this method, it is important to know that the first and last page of the text block is lost, or placed, inside the finished cover. Many different folded or sewn text blocks could be used for this cover (see Sewing with Four Needles, page 50, and Adding an Unsupported Link Stitch, page 78).

Preparing the Covers

1   Lay the outer cover paper facedown on the table surface. Place the binder's board on top of the outer cover (same height, but wider). Line up the board flush with the head and tail, and with equal spacing on each side (the foredges).

2   Use one hand to stabilize the board, then score
▼   both edges and fold the paper over the binder's board. Repeat the same steps for the other outer cover.

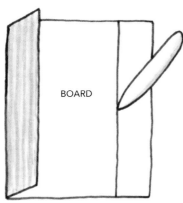

3   Lay the inner cover paper facedown on the table surface. Remove the board from the outer cover sheet and place on the inner cover sheet (same width, but taller). Line up the board flush from left to right and centered between the head and tail of the paper.

4 Score and fold over in the same manner as the
▼ outer cover. Repeat the above procedure for the
second inner sheet.

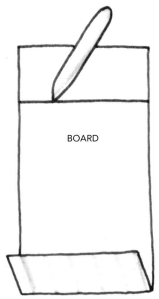

BOARD

Assembling the Covers

I Place the board back into the outer cover sheet (same height, but wider).

2 Lay the text block down with the sewn edge next
▼ to the cover's right side.

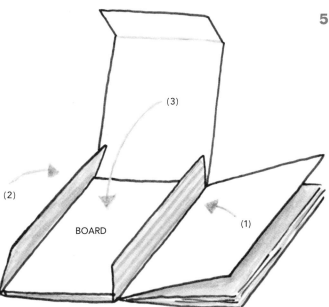

(3)

(2)

BOARD

(1)

3 Open the first sheet of the text block and place under the opposite tab. Place the tab of the inner cover between the board and outside sheet so that it wraps around the inside of the cover. This hides the first sheet of the text block and the tabs of the outside sheet.

4 Trim the corners of the tab for the other end and
▼ carefully roll into the space between the board and outside cover sheet. This may require a little effort if a heavy weight cover stock was used. Be patient and slowly slide the tab into place.

5 Close the text block and repeat the same procedure for the other side. It is important to close the text block or else it wraps around the cover and makes the inside cover show on the outside of the book.

Making the Spine

1 Pinch the covers and measure only the text block. Use that distance to prepare a spine for the book.

2 Double-score the center of the paper by using
▶ the measurement of the thickness of the text block (see Scoring the Paper, page 23). This compensates for the thickness of the text block. Do not add the thickness of the covers or the paper spine will be too large and fall out when placed on a bookshelf between other books. Trim the corners if necessary and slip over the spine (sewn edge) of the text block in between the front and back covers.

Alternative Simple Bindings

THREE-HOLE PAMPHLET

Try sewing three stations instead of the five-hole pamphlet for smaller books and a different look. The text block may be doubled in thickness by sewing two signatures simultaneously, end to end. The sewing stations must line up perfectly to work properly. *Note:* This method does not work with the wraparound cover.

RUBBER BAND AND STICK/STRAW

Loop the rubber band through a pair of holes set toward the outside ends of the text block. Carefully slip the stick or straw through the loops of the rubber band on each end to secure.

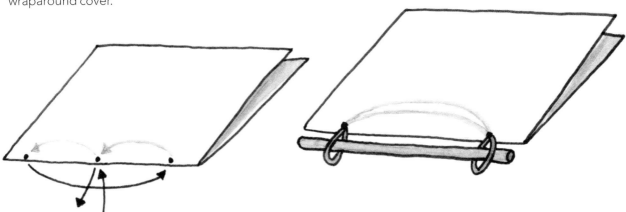

FORMULA FOR THE MATERIALS

Text Block HEIGHT and WIDTH = six signatures or more, folded to same size

Cover HEIGHT = height of signature plus 2 × square (head and tail)

WIDTH = 2 × width of signature, plus 2 × square, plus 2 × tab

Thread LENGTH = 1 × height for each signature used

MATERIALS

eight 10$\frac{1}{2}$" × 15$\frac{1}{4}$" (26.7 × 38.7 cm) folded signatures (octavos) of lightweight paper for the text block

two 5$\frac{3}{8}$" × 10" (13.7 × 25.4 cm) pieces medium to heavy weight paper for the covers

four 24" (61 cm) lengths colored linen thread for sewing

SEWING
with Four Needles

THIS IS A WONDERFUL STITCH THAT is much easier than it sounds. Four needles, thread, and paper are all that is needed to complete this beautiful exposed binding. The decorative stitch is enhanced when different colored threads are used, creating a braided or candy cane effect as it travels along the spine.

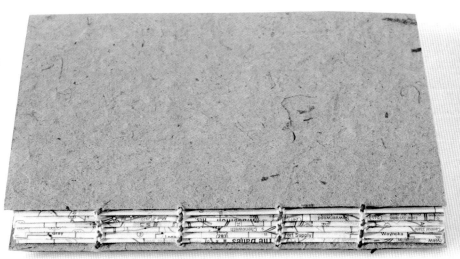

Preparing the Signatures

1 Fold the signatures to the same size. If using folios, nest them together, one inside the other, and jog the sheets until they are flush. Use a clothespin or paper clip to secure the folios (see Orientation and Signatures, page 24).

2 Use a jig to create the sewing stations for the signatures (see Multiple Signatures and Creating a Jig, page 27). Mark ¹/₂" (1.3 cm) from the head and tail for each pair of holes for greater stability. Make four holes, or two pairs of sewing stations, for each signature. Save two signatures so that they can be nested inside each cover.

Making the Cover

1 Cut the cover paper to the appropriate size and fold in half.

2 Score 1" (2.5 cm) from the open ends and fold.
▼

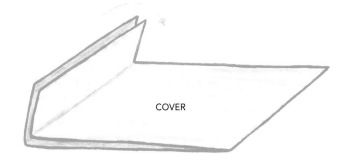

COVER

3 Punch the sewing stations for the signatures first, then place one signature inside the tab of the folded cover. Center evenly between the head and tail, and repunch the holes to include the cover. Repeat for the other cover.

Sewing the Text Block

1 Thread the four needles individually and secure (see Securing the Thread, page 28).

2 Tie and knot two of the threads together at the loose ends to use for the first pair of sewing stations. Repeat for the other two threads to use in the second pair of sewing stations.

3 ▼ Begin with one pair of threads. On the inside of the first signature that is nested inside the cover, take the first needle through the first sewing station and pull through to the outside. Take the second needle and exit the adjacent sewing station. The knot may be centered or aligned over one of the sewing stations. Repeat for the second set of sewing stations with the other two threads. *Note:* The needle goes through each sewing station twice except for the first and last signature. Keep the stitching tight and try not to pierce the thread during sewing.

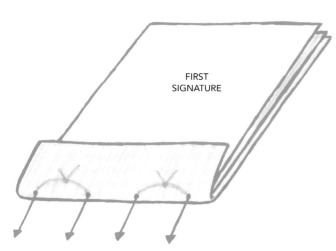

FIRST
SIGNATURE

4 ▼ With each needle, sew through the second signature by entering the sewing stations that are directly above the sewing stations you just exited.

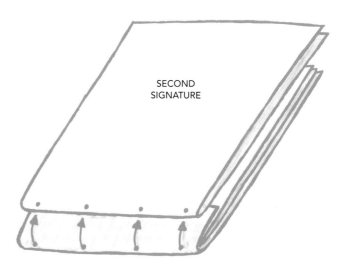

SECOND
SIGNATURE

▼ Exit each needle through the second sewing station (for that pair). All needles should then be on the outside of that signature. The threads cross each other for each pair on the inside of the signature.

5
▼ Repeat the same process for each signature by crossing over for each pair of sewing stations. Each signature is added in the same way except for the last signature, which is nested into the cover.

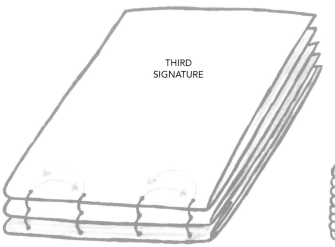

THIRD
SIGNATURE

6
▼ Finish with all four needles on the inside of the last signature and cover. Make the two threads rest over one of the sewing stations to ensure a tighter knot. Tie a square knot and trim off any extra thread to $1/4$" (6 mm).

FORMULA FOR THE MATERIALS

Text Block   HEIGHT = desired finished height

WIDTH = 8 × desired folded width

Cards   HEIGHT = height of text block

WIDTH = width of one accordion panel

Cover   HEIGHT = height of folded accordion plus 2 × square (head and tail)

WIDTH = width of folded accordion plus 1 × square (foredge)

MATERIALS

one 5" × 22 ½" (12.7 × 57.2 cm) piece medium weight paper for the folded text block

six 5" × 2 ¾" (12.7 × 7 cm) pieces medium weight paper for the cards

two 5⅛" × 2 ⅞" (13 × 7.3 cm) pieces binder's board for the covers

ACCORDION
with Woven Panels

ACCORDIONS ARE ONE OF THE MOST widely used constructions in making artist's books. Accordions have a playful and versatile quality both in size and format. Accordions encourage the viewer to investigate the panels as individual pages or as an elongated series. Variations are also illustrated throughout this section. Accordions are great to use in combination with different binding methods or just to alter the shape of a structure. Sewing onto a peak or gutter or utilizing one of the single folded elements discussed in this section are interesting ways to create a truly unique structure.

The following demonstrates how to fold an even eight-panel accordion from one sheet of paper. Choose a paper large or long enough to maximize the size. Large-format accordions can be made by hinging or joining several sheets together (see Tipping On and Hinging Panels, page 35).

Folding the Text Block

1 ▼ Fold the long sheet of paper in half and open.

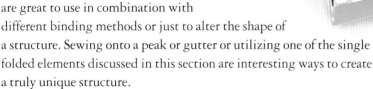

2 ▼ Take one loose end and line it up to the gutter and fold. Repeat for the other side.

3 ▼ Take one of the loose ends and align toward the outside fold that was just created. Repeat for the other side.

Cutting and Weaving the Text Block

4 Flip over the folded sheet, take the folded edge,
▼ and align toward the original center fold. Repeat for the other side. This finishes the accordion and ensures eight even panels without having to reverse any folds.

I Cut three lines between the second and seventh
▼ panels along the length of the accordion across the folds. Either a straight or curved line may be used.

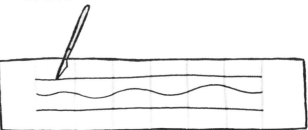

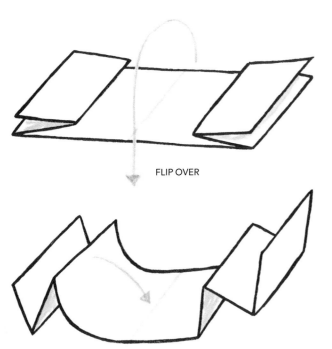

FLIP OVER

2 To weave the first card, go in and out of each slat until it reaches the bottom of that panel. The card should fit tightly on all edges for each panel.

3 The second card is woven through the opposite sides of the first card. Start on the opposite side of the accordion panel, weaving in and out of each slat until it reaches the bottom of the panel. This secures the second and third panels on the accordion.

4 Continue in the same way for the remaining
▼ panels by altering the weaving pattern for each new card.

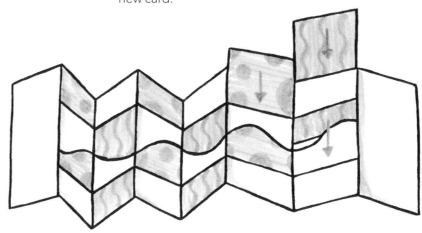

Single Hard Cover (Constructing the Covers)

1 Carefully measure the height and width of the text block. Use a smaller square of $^1/_{16}$" (1.6 mm) at the head, tail, and foredge for the cover to prevent the text block from sagging when the book is displayed open. When gluing, the cover should be flush to the spine of the text block to keep the covers from knocking onto one another (see Cutting Down the Materials, page 20).

2 Glue the cover with a mixture of two-thirds PVA to one-third methyl cellulose and press onto the back side of the paper or cloth. Clip the corners and turn in the edges (see Turning Over the Edges, page 36).

3 Glue the back of one end panel on the accordion. They act as the end sheets. Carefully line up the loose end so the square is even for the head, tail, and foredge, and press onto the back of the front cover. The back folded edge of the text block should be flush to the edge of the cover. This prevents the boards from knocking up on one another as the book is opened. Repeat for the back cover in the same manner and press the book until completely dry.

Alternative Accordions

POP-UP WINDOW ACCORDION

The pop-up window accordion creates a structure that when folded back with the covers touching is called a carousel book. Once again, using the eight-panel accordion as a guide, the second or top piece of paper is the same height, but 1" to 2" (2.5 to 5.1 cm) shorter in length. Fold both pieces the same way. Cut or tear out windows along the four folded edges of the shorter sheet. Lay the larger sheet of paper so that the loose ends are pointing up. Tip on an adhesive to the three center peaks and the loose ends to secure the second sheet. The window creates depth and mystery. Additional layers may be added as long as the subsequent sheets are shorter in length.

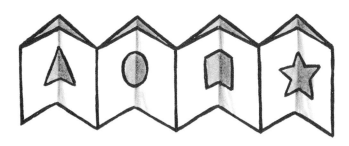

ACCORDION WITH POCKET

The accordion with a pocket is a great way to house postcards, photographs, and any other memorabilia. The height of the paper needs to be adjusted to allow for the pocket to be folded up from the bottom. Add the amount for the desired pocket height to the height of the paper. Fold the pocket over first. Make sure the pocket is facedown, and then proceed with folding the eight-panel accordion as shown above. Tip on an adhesive to the loose ends of the pocket on the first and eighth panel to secure.

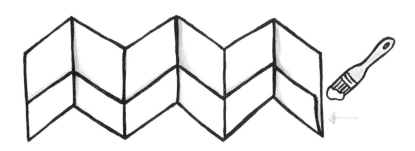

FORMULA FOR THE MATERIALS

Text Block   HEIGHT and WIDTH = 4 X folded size, square sheets

Cover   HEIGHT and WIDTH = folded accordion plus 2 X square (head, tail, and foredges)

MATERIALS

five 5" × 5" (12.7 × 12.7 cm) pieces lightweight paper for the text block

two 2¹/₂" × 2¹/₂" (6.4 × 6.4 cm) pieces colored heavy cover weight paper for the covers

STAR ACCORDION

EVERY AGE SEEMS TO ENJOY THE PLAYFUL QUALITY OF this book. The pages are easy to prepare and construct. The only rule is that the paper must be square and each sheet cut to the same size.

Each page is composed of three simple folds. In origami the completed shape is called the lotus fold because of its flower shape. This is a starter fold for many origami constructions. The method shown below demonstrates how to fold without reversing any of the folds. Five sheets work best for this structure. This versatile book, however, may be adapted to make ornaments, garlands, note cards, or pop-ups.

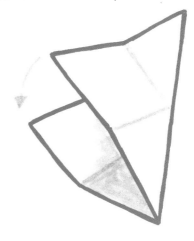

Folding the Text Block

I ▼ With the image side of the paper faceup, fold the piece of paper in half.

3 ▼ Open the paper and flip the sheet over. The third and final fold should go against the other two folds. This avoids having to reverse any of the folds. Fold diagonally from one corner to the opposite corner and stop.

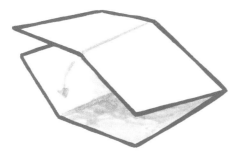

2 ▼ Open and turn the paper 90 degrees. Then fold the paper in half in the other direction (visually this equals four squares).

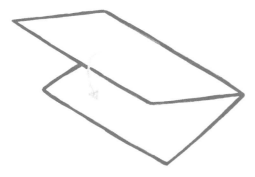

4 Prop the piece of paper so that the peak or folded edge is faceup. Push in the center of the paper until it touches the table and pops. Doing so reverses the folds automatically and creates a lotus shape.

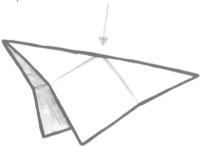

5 Visually, the paper has two squares and four triangles on the surface. To close the lotus, put one hand on the square shape and grab the opposite square with the other hand until they meet.

6 Repeat the steps above for the four remaining sheets.

7 Separate the folded sheets into two piles—three in one and two in the other.

8 *Pile of three:* With the folded edges faceup, lightly draw an X on the top corner on both sides. Repeat for the other two sheets.

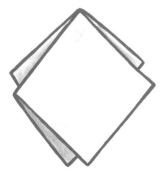

9 *Pile of two:* With the open end faceup, lightly draw an O on the top corner on both sides. Repeat for the second sheet.

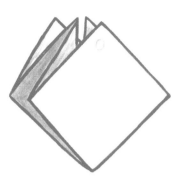

10 Take one of the "X" sheets and glue the surface with a mixture of two-thirds PVA to one-third methyl cellulose. Be careful not to let any adhesive spill over the edges. This keeps the pages from sticking together. Pick up the folded sheet from the "O" pile and make the X "kiss" the O. Continue by alternating the sheets in the same way until all five sheets have been glued together (X, O, X, O, X). This allows the book to open flat.

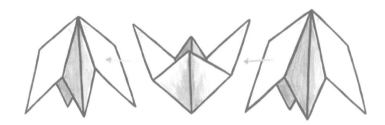

TIP By gluing the folded edges together instead of alternating, the book only opens as a star. Single lotus folds could also be used as individual pop-ups between pages.

11 The covers should be at least the same size if not larger than the closed book. Giving an even square for all four edges is recommended. Cover with paper or cloth and turn in the edges (see Turning Over the Edges, page 36). Glue the end sheet of the text block and center onto the cover. Repeat the process for the other cover. Press the book until completely dry.

Spiral and Zigzag
ACCORDIONS

THIS IS ANOTHER GREAT IDEA FOR A POCKET-SIZED accordion. The paper can be either square or rectangular in shape. The finished result is one-eighth of the original size, maintaining the same shape. The wonderful thing about this book is that it may be opened in any direction. Different pages are exposed depending on the orientation of the book. The spiral accordion book is shown at right; the zigzag version is shown on page 62.

Folding the Text Block

1 Fold the piece of paper in half. *Note:* It does not matter which side is folded first because it is also folded in the other direction (see Folding Paper, page 23).

2 Take one of the loose ends and fold back toward ▼ the first folded edge. Then flip over the paper and repeat for the other side. This makes a four-panel accordion.

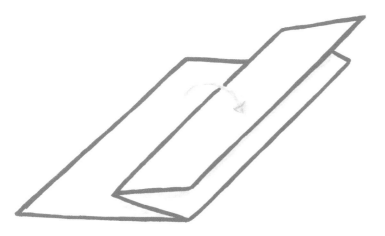

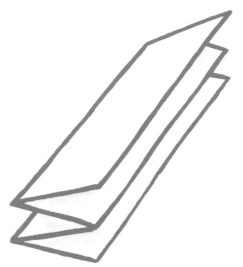

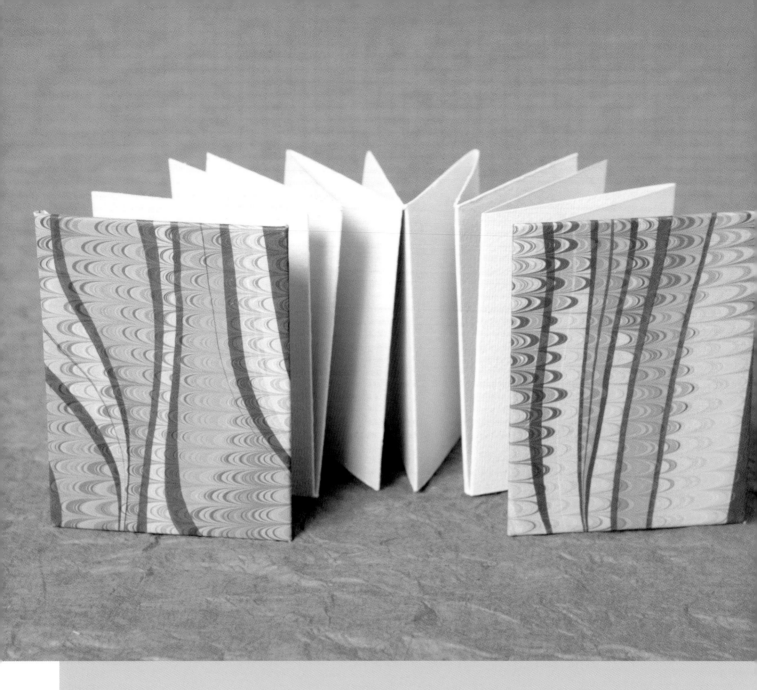

FORMULA FOR THE MATERIALS

Text Block   HEIGHT and WIDTH = 4 × desired finished size

Cover   HEIGHT and WIDTH = folded accordion plus 2 × square (head, tail, and foredges)

MATERIALS

Spiral   one 9" × 9" (22.9 × 22.9 cm) piece light to medium weight paper for the text block

two 2³⁄₈" × 2³⁄₈" (6 × 6 cm) pieces binder's board for the covers

Zigzag   one 9" × 12" (22.9 × 30.5 cm) piece light to medium weight paper for the text block

two 3¹⁄₈" × 2³⁄₈" (7.9 × 6 cm) pieces binder's board for the covers

3 Open flat and turn the sheet of paper 90 degrees.

▼ Fold the piece of paper the same way in steps 1 and 2.

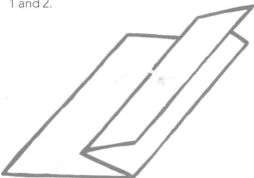

4 Open the paper so that it lies flat, visually creating sixteen squares or rectangles.

Cutting the Text Block

1 For easier cutting, draw a path along the folded edges. The patterns can be altered; it is important, however, that each accordion panel is attached to the adjacent panel. Otherwise the panels fall apart into individual sheets. Choose one of the following patterns to complete the text block.

▼ SPIRAL PATTERN

This creates a spiral of connected panels.

- Start one square from the bottom left edge and draw a line up three squares.
- Draw a line over two squares toward the right.
- Draw a line down two squares toward the bottom.
- Draw a line over one square toward the left.
- Draw a line up one square toward the top, ending in the center of the paper.

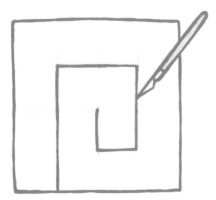

▼ ZIGZAG PATTERN

This creates a M or W shape.

- Start one square from the bottom left edge and draw a line up three squares.
- Go to the center top edge and draw a line down three squares.
- Go one square from the bottom right edge and draw a line up three squares.

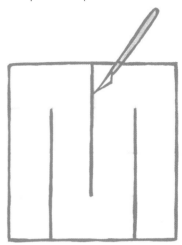

2 Carefully cut along the drawn lines with a craft knife and ruler.

3 To fold the accordion, hold one of the loose ends in one hand and start to fold one square on top of the next. Some folds need to be reversed as the pattern continues. It is important to make sure that each panel folds over easily. The pages should not wrap around one another.

4 Create a cover with a square on all four edges. Cover the board as desired (see Turning Over the Edges, page 36).

5 Glue the back side of one end panel and smooth. This functions as the end sheet of the text block and is centered onto the back side of the cover. Repeat for the other cover. Press the book until completely dry.

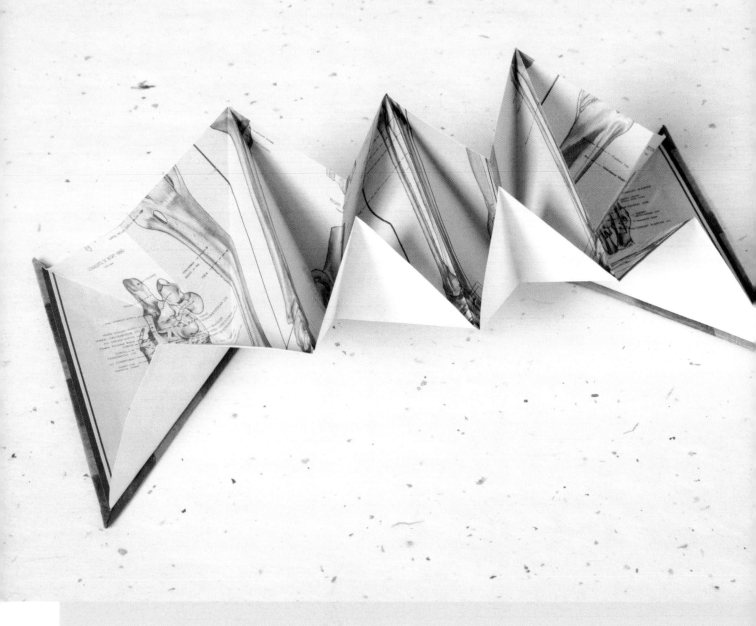

FORMULA FOR THE MATERIALS

Text Block   HEIGHT = finished book size

WIDTH = 4 × height (for an eight-panel accordion)

Cover   HEIGHT and WIDTH = folded accordion plus 1 × square for all three edges

MATERIALS

one 5" × 20" (12.7 × 50.8 cm) piece light to medium weight paper for the text block

two 5¹⁄₂" × 2³⁄₄" (14 × 7 cm) pieces binder's board for the covers

Triangle ACCORDION

THIS BEAUTIFUL AND UNIQUELY SHAPED BOOK is a nice departure from the more traditional square or rectangle. The eight-panel accordion is the starting point for this triangular book, but quickly takes on a different shape with some additional folding.

Folding the Text Block

1 Fold the sheet of paper into an eight-panel accordion (see Accordion with Woven Panels, page 54).

2 ▼ Place the folded paper so that the four peaks are all faceup. Starting at one end, take one folded edge and fold it over so that the folded corner meets up with the gutter of the panel. Repeat for the opposite side to create a triangular shape.

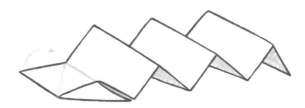

3 Open both of the triangular folds and fold back toward the other side so that the paper is more flexible, then fold back to a flat position.

4 ▼ Open the panel and reverse the triangular folds so they push forward to the opposite side.

REVERSE FOLD

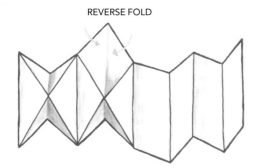

5 ▼ Repeat the same steps for the remaining three folded edges. When complete, this creates a 45/45/90-degree triangle.

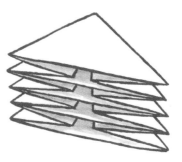

Creating the Covers

1 Covers are made into the same triangular shape. Adding ¹⁄₈" (3 mm) to all three sides is recommended for the square. The corners for the turnovers on the 45-degree angled side need to be at a sharper angle so that they do not overlap the edge. A 30-degree angle is recommended for both sides to create a more mitered corner. Remember to come at least one board's thickness from the corners to avoid exposing the board.

2 Turn over the edges one at a time. When pinching the corners down, pinch toward the adjacent side to avoid excessively pointy corners.

3 Glue the back side of the end sheet. Center the text block onto the cover and smooth. Repeat for the other cover and press the book until dry.

FORMULA FOR THE MATERIALS

Text Block	HEIGHT = finished book size
	WIDTH = finished book size (folios may be substituted, 2 × width finished book size)
Cover	HEIGHT = height of book plus ⅝" (1.6 cm) for both head and tail
	WIDTH = width of book plus ⅝" (1.6 cm) for spine and foredges
Tissue paper	HEIGHT and WIDTH = 1" × 6" (2.5 × 15.2 cm)
Corner Tabs	HEIGHT and WIDTH = 1" × 1" (2.5 × 2.5 cm)
Thread	LENGTH = 6 × height of text block
Paste Label	HEIGHT and WIDTH = typically ¼ to ⅕ of actual cover size

MATERIALS

twelve 4¾" × 12½" (12.1 × 31.8 cm) pieces lightweight paper for the text block

two 6" × 7½" (15.2 × 19.1 cm) pieces light to medium weight paper for the covers

two 1" × 6" (2.5 × 15.2 cm) pieces Japanese tissue paper for the inner binding

two 1" × 1" (2.5 × 2.5 cm) pieces decorative paper for the corner tabs

one 30" (76.2 cm) length linen thread for sewing

one 1" × 4" (2.5 × 10.2 cm) piece scrap paper for the paste label

CROSS SIDE STITCH

(Stab Binding)

A STAB BINDING IS A WONDERFUL WAY TO BIND SINGLE SHEETS. THE SPINE IS EXPOSED, showing off the various patterns. This structure functions like a flip book rather than opening completely flat as with other sewing methods. The cross stitch is the focus for this section. However, additional patterns are shown at the end of this section. Try them all or create one of your own!

The stab binding is also referred to as a Japanese side stitch. However, there are Chinese and Korean versions that are similar in appearance. Japanese books are bound with either four or five points or sewing stations. The Chinese style has four sewing stations while the Korean style has five sewing stations.

Preparing the Text Block

Single sheets, or leaves, may be used for the text block. If folios are used instead of individual leafs, make sure that each folio is stacked on top of the next and not nested inside one another. Having the folded edge flush to the foredge is a nice way of doubling the thickness of each page, yielding half the amount of pages. The folded edge, however, may also be aligned along the spine edge for a different look.

> **TIP** For a thicker text block, try using a drill to create the holes. The drill removes the material rather than pushing it toward the back of the text block.

Creating the Inner Binding

One of the most important steps in putting the book together is the inner binding. Although this step can be omitted, it is recommended so that the book does not come apart if the exposed stitching fails or becomes damaged. The inner binding also strengthens and holds the text block in place without the use of weights or clips during sewing.

1   Gather, knock up, and align all the pages. Clip together with clothespins to secure.

2   Measure and mark four holes about $^1/_4"$ (6 mm) from the spine edge to make two pairs of holes; each pair should be evenly spaced, about one-third of the way in from the head and tail. There should be no more than 1" (2.5 cm) between the pairs of holes. Punch the holes with an awl on a punching board all the way through to create a large enough hole to encompass the twisted paper (see Punching Sewing Stations, page 26).

Creating the Corner Tabs

3 Starting from one corner, twist the thin Japanese
▼ paper at a slight angle all the way to the bottom
to form a string. Thread each end of the twisted
paper through the first pair of punched holes from
the front side to the back. Repeat for the second
piece of paper.

TWIST

1 The corner pieces are traditionally made of silk.
▼ Although primarily decorative, they protect the
corners from damage. Cut the two corner tabs.
Fold the 1" (2.5 cm) corner tabs in half to ensure
an even ½" (1.3 cm) coverage on each side of
the corners. Paste the corner tabs perpendicular
to the fold. Pinch with your fingers to ensure a
tight fit and let the tabs dry completely before
proceeding to the next step. Since the corner
tabs extend from the text block on both sides,
let the book hang over the edge of the table.

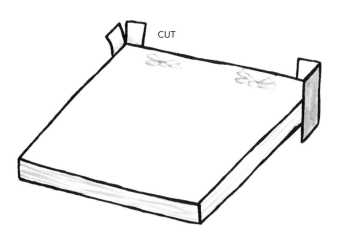

CUT

4 Tie the loose ends once and pound the knots
▼ with a mallet or hammer on both sides. This
flattens any raised material from the punching
and secures the ties. Trim off the ends so that
they do not overhang the edges.

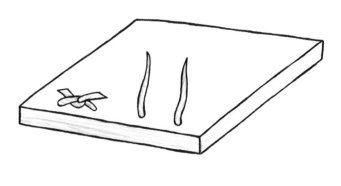

2 Slit the corner tabs along the folded edge from
▼ the text block out on both sides. Glue each
individual tab and press down, one on top of
the other, to finish the corner. Repeat for the
other corner.

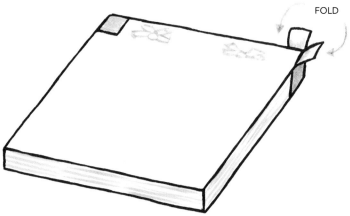

FOLD

Creating the Covers

1 Place and center the text block on the back side of one cover paper. Score the outline of the text block around all edges. This is the same as turning over the edges for hard covers, just without using binder's board.

2 Remove the text block, fold over the edges, and open back up.

3 ▼ Clip the corners at a 45-degree angle slightly away from where the score marks meet. This creates a slight overlap once the edges are turned in.

4 Paste the turn-ins with a thin line of paste and press into place. Paste works best because it does not stain the delicate papers like PVA. Repeat the process for the other cover.

5 Apply a thin line of paste along the perimeter of the back side of the cover. Place the cover on top of the text block and secure. The covers should be slightly larger than the text block, so when positioning the cover, align it flush to the spine edge and give an even amount of spacing at the head, tail, and foredge. Repeat the same steps for the other cover.

Sewing the Book

1 Mark the sewing stations ¹/₂" (1.3 cm) from the edge of the spine. Two of the sewing stations should be ¹/₂" (1.3 cm) from the head and tail. Mark the other three sewing stations as desired along the same line ¹/₂" (1.3 cm) from the spine.

2 ▼ Punch the sewing stations with an awl or drill. The needle passes through each sewing station a total of three times. Make sure the sewing stations are able to accommodate the needle and thread being used.

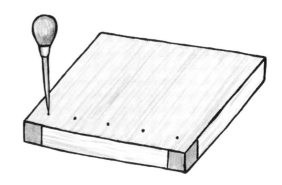

TIP Additional holes may be added to vary the look of the pattern. The instructions demonstrate a binding with five sewing stations.

3 Starting from the back side of the book, begin sewing into the first sewing station at one end and pull the string almost all the way through, leaving a 3" to 4" (7.6 to 10.2 cm) tail to tie off at the end (1).

4 ▼ Loop around the side edge and go back into the same sewing station (2). Keep the stitching tight while sewing.

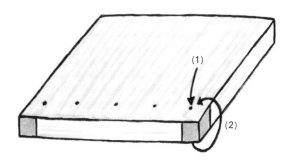

5 Wrap the string around the spine edge and go through the same sewing station for a third time. This finishes off the corner. The stitching should line up nicely with the corner tabs (3). Enter the next sewing station along the spine (4).

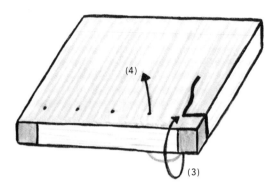

6 Wrap the thread over the spine and enter the next sewing station along the spine (5). Exit the sewing station and wrap the thread over the spine again to enter the previous sewing station for the second time (6).

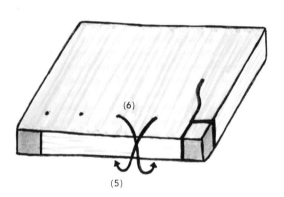

7 Sew into the next sewing station toward the unfinished end (7). This stitch is visible on the flat side of the cover. Wrap the thread around the spine edge and proceed into the next sewing station (8).

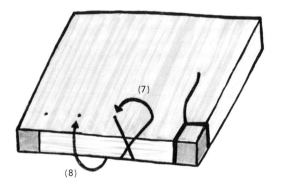

8 Wrap the thread over the spine again and enter the previous sewing station for the second time (9). Exit the sewing station and enter the next sewing station toward the unfinished end, once again visible on the flat side of the cover (10).

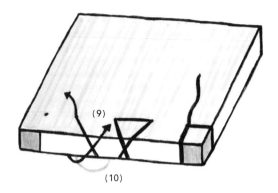

9 Sew into the last sewing station (11). Wrap the thread around the outside edge and enter the sewing station again (12). This stitch should line up with the corner tab.

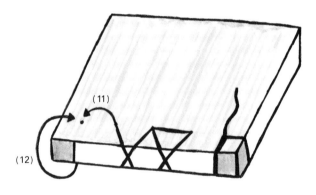

10 Wrap the thread around the spine and enter the same sewing station for a third time (13) to finish off the corner. Fill in the remaining gaps on the flat side of the covers by sewing in and out of each sewing station staying on the flat side of the covers until the second to last hole (14 and 15).

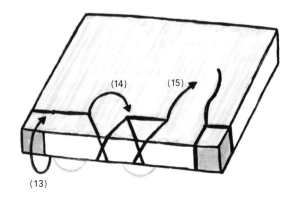

II
▼ Use the threads to tie a square knot over the first sewing station. Pull the knot into the sewing station by pushing the needle through the sewing station a fourth time. Gently pull the thread to hide the knot into the sewing station. If using a thinner text block, the knot may not slip into the sewing station. Trim the threads flush to the covers on both sides to finish.

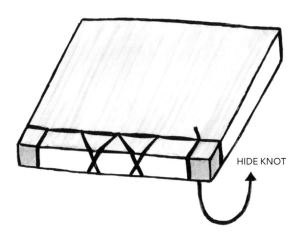

HIDE KNOT

Creating the Paste Label

A paste label, or title strip, is traditionally glued onto the front cover of the book. A scrap piece of tissue paper may be cut or torn into a long slender shape. If any writing is intended as a title, write on the paper before gluing. This is the last step in creating the stab binding and creates a nice accent.

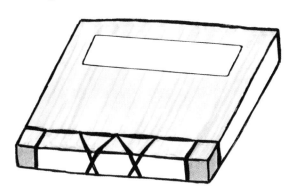

Alternative Traditional Stab Bindings

YOTSUME TOJI (Japanese Four- or Five-Hole Binding)
▼ Thread = 5 × height of text block

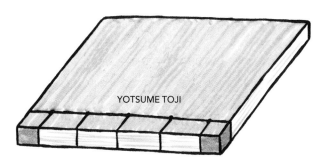

YOTSUME TOJI

KIKKO TOJI (Tortoise Shell Binding)
▼ Thread = 7 × height of text block

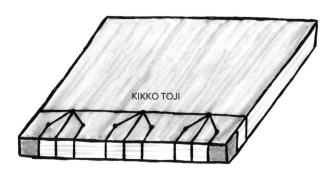

KIKKO TOJI

ASA NO HA TOJI (Hemp Leaf Binding)
▼ Thread = 7 × height of text block

ASA NO HA TOJI

FORMULA FOR THE MATERIALS

Text Block	HEIGHT = desired book size
	WIDTH = 2 × desired book size
Mull	HEIGHT = $\frac{1}{8}$" (3 mm) shorter than height of text block
	WIDTH = thickness of text block, plus 2 × turnover ($\frac{5}{8}$" [1.6 cm])
Headband	WIDTH = thickness of spine
Spine Liner	HEIGHT = $\frac{1}{8}$" (3 mm) shorter than height of text block
	WIDTH = thickness of text block
Binder's Board	HEIGHT = height of text block, plus 2 × square
	WIDTH = width of text block, plus 1 × square, minus 2 boards' thickness
Spine	HEIGHT = height of text block, plus 2 × square (same height as covers)
	WIDTH = thickness of text block, plus 2 boards' thickness

MATERIALS

ten 6" × 8$\frac{3}{4}$" (15.2 × 22.2 cm) pieces lightweight paper for the text block

one 5$\frac{7}{8}$" × 2" (14.9 × 5.1 cm) piece mull to support the text block

two $\frac{1}{4}$" (6 mm) headbands for the head and tail

one 5$\frac{7}{8}$" × $\frac{1}{4}$" (14.9 cm × 6 mm) piece tissue paper for the spine liner on the text block

two 6$\frac{1}{4}$" × 4$\frac{5}{16}$" (15.9 × 11 cm) pieces binder's board for the cover

one 6$\frac{1}{4}$" × $\frac{5}{16}$" (15.9 cm × 8 mm) piece binder's board for the spine

PERFECT BINDING

"NECESSITY IS THE MOTHER OF INVENTION." This binding style was created because of the image design in the book. The images filled the entire page and a line of text ran through the gutter of each folio. Sewing on top of the folio would have taken away from the image and legibility of the text. A double-sided adhesive tape was used instead of sewing to secure the pages. The final design layout for this structure was cleaner and much less complicated to bind.

Perfect-bound structures typically refer to the binding of single pages on one edge of the leaf of paper. Similar to a paper tablet with tear-off sheets, this structure is not very stable and will wear out faster than a folded sheet. I adapted this method to suit my needs. A heavier paper stock works well for the text block.

Building the Text Block

I   With the image side faceup, create the folios for the text block. The backs of each folio are glued during construction.

TIP   Using a double-sided adhesive tape works better for this project because it does not add any moisture. If pages are printed on an ink-jet printer, the ink is unforgiving when it comes in contact with any amount of water. If any sticking occurs from an adhesive, the toner often lifts or flakes off the printer paper.

2   For the first folio, cut two pieces of double-sided
▼   tape slightly shorter than the height of the folio (see Adhesives, page 31). The tape runs parallel to the folded edge and the foredge of each folio. Peel the backing off of the tape and place it along the spine and foredge of the folio. *Note:* A thin line of adhesive (two-thirds PVA to one-third methyl cellulose) may be used instead of the double-sided tape. Be careful that no adhesive spills over the edge.

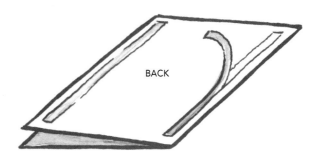

BACK

3 Peel off the backing of the strip of tape along the
▼ spine edge of the folio and carefully place the new
folio so that the folded edges are flush. Once the
folded edge is secured, peel the backing off of
the tape for the foredge. Let the back side of the
new folio rest neatly on top and press firmly.

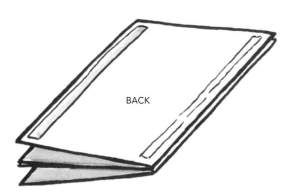

BACK

4 Repeat the same steps for all of the other folios
to build up the text block. The tape along the
two edges is enough to secure the entire sheet.
A heavier adhesive is used to secure the entire
end sheet onto the cover.

Reinforcing the Spine

GLUING THE SPINE

1 Tape a separate piece of wax paper over the
▼ edges of two boards. Sandwich the text block
between the two boards. The spine of the text
block should be flush with the edge of the boards.

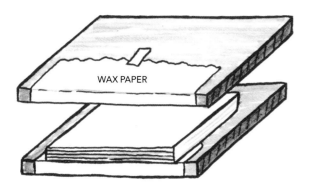

WAX PAPER

2 Place a weight on top and glue the spine with
▼ pure PVA. Work the adhesive between each folio.
Allow it to dry for at least one hour, to overnight.
Once dry, take the text block out from between
the boards and remove any excess dried glue.

WEIGHT

MULL

1 *Mull*, or *super*, is a starched cheesecloth material
▼ that is used to reinforce the text block. Cut a
piece of mull and glue the spine again with PVA.
Carefully smooth the mull over the spine. Glue the
mull turn-ins onto the backs of each end page.

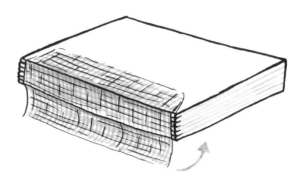

TIP When a book falls apart, the inner
binding may be visible. Often, the mull holds
up better than the sewn text block, which is
an ideal area for reinforcement. A piece of thin
cotton or linen cloth may be used instead of
mull for support.

HEADBANDS

Headbands are traditionally sewn into the text block before gluing the spine. Since this structure has no sewing, a decorative headband is made with a heavy cotton string and scrap paper or book cloth.

1 ▼ Cut a strip of book cloth 1" × 4" (2.5 × 10.2 cm) and a cotton string longer than the strip of cloth.

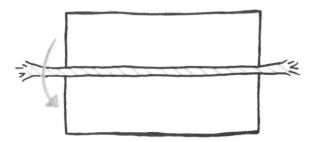

2 ▼ Glue the back side of the cloth and fold it over the string. Bone-fold the overlap and push the string up as far as it can go to create a nice rounded edge. Let it dry for fifteen to thirty minutes. Save the leftover headbands to use on other projects.

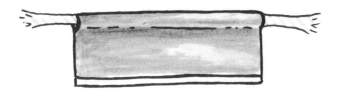

TIP Headbands may be purchased by the yard at stores that specialize in bookbinding supplies. They come in a variety of colors and are used for decoration. The traditional purpose of the headband is to give additional support at the head. A book is typically pulled off of the shelf by grabbing the headband, creating stress to the spine of the book. In contemporary binding, the adhesives are strong, so a reinforced sewn headband is not always necessary.

3 Cut a headband for the head and tail. The colored top of the head and tail bands should gently roll over the text block. Commercial headbands have a stronger colored side; make sure this is facing out toward the foredge of the text block. Glue with pure PVA to the spine of the text block.

SPINE LINER

1 Cut a spine liner from tissue paper. These thinner papers are strong when dry and keep the glued spine from sticking to the inside of the cover.

2 ▼ Glue the strip of tissue paper, center, and gently smooth over the spine. This completes the text block.

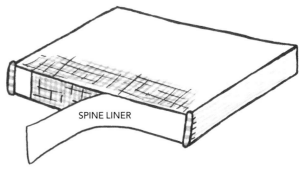

SPINE LINER

Making the Cover

1 Cut the two pieces of board for the front and back cover.

2 For the spine, sandwich the text block between the cover boards and squeeze tightly. Measure at the spine and foredge. Take the average of the two measurements to determine the width of the spine. It is best to make the spine a little shorter in width than the board and text block because the cloth adds bulk when covered. If this is not done, then the wider spine will not allow the book to slide on and off of the shelf as easily.

Covering the Boards

1 The average joint width is approximately $^3/_8$" (1 cm). Use the formula below when using non-traditional materials or the book will not function as well. *Note:* Book cloth is recommended for any joint spacing because of the wear and tear from repeatedly opening the book. This causes a lot of stress to the hinge and paper does not last as long.

FORMULA FOR THE JOINT SPACER

Joint width = two boards, plus 2 × cloth thickness, plus 1 × square

2 Tape may be used to simulate the joint spacing and to test the boards before covering. If any of the calculations are off, recut the boards to the appropriate size. The spine of the text block overlaps the joint spacer when an even square is given at the head, tail, and foredge. This is necessary so that the book is flexible enough to open flat.

3 Cut a piece of book cloth 1" (2.5 cm) larger all the way around to include the covers, spine, joint spacers, and turn-ins.

4 Glue the front cover first with a mixture of two-thirds PVA to one-third methyl cellulose onto the back side of the material on the left side. Flip over and smooth the other side (see Gluing the Materials, page 34).

5 Use a straight edge or ruler to align the spine. Measure the joint space (around $^3/_8$" [1 cm]), glue the board for the spine, and place to the right of the front cover. Check the measurement at the top as well to be certain that the spine is parallel to the front cover.

6 ▼ Measure the same joint space to the right of the spine strip (around $^3/_8$" [1 cm]). Glue the back cover and smooth the face side as before.

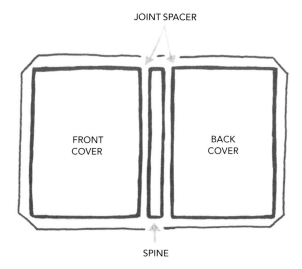

JOINT SPACER

FRONT COVER   BACK COVER

SPINE

7 Use the cheater's strip to trim excess cloth around all the edges (see Tools, page 15). Trim and turn in the edges on the head and tail (see Turning Over the Edges, page 36). Press the cloth into the joint space. The turn-in will not be flush to the inside edges of the joint spacer, but the back side of the fabric should touch. If forced, the fabric or paper may ear.

8 Test the cover by placing the text block inside before casing in the text block. The term *casing in* is used for gluing the text block into the cover. Casing in from the front to the back is advisable because the placement is cleaner and easier. The front is also the first thing that is seen and should be as neat as possible.

9 Place waste paper that is larger than the text block
▼ inside the end page and glue with the adhesive mixture. Remove the waste paper and place the text block in at an angle, starting at the foredge, onto the front cover. The spine edge of the text block should hang over the joint spacer. This is normal and allows for greater flexibility when opening the book. Open the text block slightly to smooth any wrinkles or air bubbles, working from the foredge to the gutter of the end page. Do not open the text block too much or else it may slide out of position.

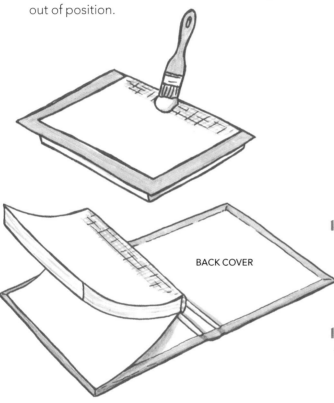

BACK COVER

TIP Thin knitting needles, barbeque skewers, or the flat part of a metal hanger may also be used to enhance the joint spacer. A flat piece of metal may be screwed onto the edge of a board so it rises above the surface. This is used in professional binderies.

10 Do not glue the spine for this structure! This
▼ decreases the flexibility of the text block and defeats the purpose of adding on the spine liner. Place waste paper inside the end page for the back cover and glue. Remove the waste paper. This time, lift the cover so that the spine is perpendicular to the table surface. Gently lay the cover on top of the glued end sheet, visually lining up the back cover with the front cover in all directions.

END SHEET

11 Gently flip over the book and smooth out the end page from the foredge to the gutter as before. Resist the urge to open the book. Allow the book to dry completely because it may pull up the spine edge of the end sheet.

12 Bone-fold along the joint space to enhance the
▼ gap, and to create what is called a *French groove*. To reinforce this groove, tie a heavy string along the joint spacer. Make sure the knot is at the end of the text block as to not create any indentions when pressing.

13 Press between two boards and apply weight. Allow the book to dry for several hours or overnight. Remove the string and the book is complete.

FORMULA FOR THE MATERIALS

Signatures	HEIGHT = desired book size
	WIDTH = desired book size
End Papers	HEIGHT = height of text block
	WIDTH = 2 × width of text block
Thread	LENGTH = 6 × height of text block
Mull	HEIGHT = $\frac{1}{8}$" (3 mm) shorter than text block
	WIDTH = thickness of spine, plus $\frac{5}{8}$" (1.6 cm) for both sides
Headband	WIDTH = thickness of spine
Spine Liner	HEIGHT = $\frac{1}{16}$" (1.6 mm) shorter than text block
	WIDTH = thickness of spine
Binder's Board	HEIGHT = height of text block plus 2 × square
	WIDTH = width of text block plus 1 × square, minus 2 boards' thickness
Spine	HEIGHT = height of cover boards
	WIDTH = thickness of text block plus 2 boards' thickness

MATERIALS

six 19$\frac{1}{2}$" × 27$\frac{1}{2}$" (49.5 × 69.9 cm) folded signatures (octavos) of lightweight paper for the text block

two 9$\frac{1}{2}$" × 13" (24.1 × 33 cm) pieces light to medium weight paper for the end papers

one 70" (177.8 cm) piece linen thread for sewing

one 9$\frac{3}{8}$" × 2" (23.8 × 5.1 cm) piece mull to support the text block

two $\frac{1}{2}$" (1.3 cm) headbands for the head and tail

one 9$\frac{1}{4}$" × $\frac{1}{2}$" (23.5 × 1.3 cm) piece tissue paper for the spine liner on the text block

two 9$\frac{3}{4}$" × 6$\frac{7}{16}$" (24.8 × 16.4 cm) pieces binder's board for the cover

one 9$\frac{3}{4}$" × $\frac{5}{8}$" (24.8 × 1.6 cm) piece binder's board for the spine

Flat Back
JOURNAL

THE FLAT BACK JOURNAL IS AN IMPORTANT AND fundamental book because it encompasses many different techniques. After making this book, the skills acquired enable the artist to troubleshoot on more complicated structures. This project covers folding multiple signatures, sewing, supporting, and reinforcing the text block, and creating a hard cover with an inset.

Preparing the Signatures

Quartos and octavos work best as the signatures so that no clips are needed to hold the pages together during sewing (see Orientation and Signatures, page 24). Any number of signatures may be used for this binding. If folios are used instead of the self-contained signatures, make sure that each gathering of folios is clipped separately with no more than six sheets of paper for each signature.

Sewing Multiple Signatures with an Unsupported Link Stitch

The length of thread is based on the height of the text block multiplied by the number of signatures (add one extra length for safe measure). If the thread is too long, measure the thread by holding one end with one hand and stretch to the opposite shoulder. This is how experienced bookbinders measure their thread, because it is a more comfortable amount to use in proportion to the binder's own body. It may require joining a new thread once the length of the old thread has expired (see Weaver's Knot, page 29).

1   Prepare six or more signatures to the desired size.

2   Create a jig with eight sewing stations in the following pattern: a single hole ¹/₂" (1.3 cm) from each end, three pairs of sewing stations evenly spaced between the single sewing stations (see Multiple Signatures and Creating a Jig, page 27). The pairs of sewing stations should be at least ¹/₂" (1.3 cm) apart to make sewing easier. More or fewer pairs of sewing stations may be used, depending on the size of the book. It is important that there is an even amount of sewing stations for this stitch.

3   Punch the sewing stations for each signature (see Punching Sewing Stations, page 26).

FIRST SIGNATURE

1 ▼ As a preliminary note, the needle passes through each sewing station once for this stitch. Begin on the outside of the first signature. Sew in and out of each sewing station, ending on the outside of the signature. Having the thread on the outside enables the sewer to tie a knot at the end of the second signature.

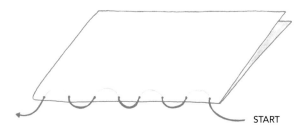

START

SECOND SIGNATURE

1 Lay the second signature on top of the first signature. Sew into the sewing station of the new signature. Exit the next sewing station and pick up the thread (stitch) from the signature directly below. Enter the next sewing station to link the two signatures together. Continue in the same way along the spine. Exit the last sewing station and stay on the outside of the signature.

2 ▼ Tighten the thread in the same direction of the sewing. Tie the loose threads twice to make a square knot. Bone-fold the sewn edge of the signature so that it lies flat. This maintains the shape as each signature is added.

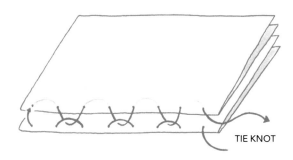

TIE KNOT

THIRD AND ALL OTHER SIGNATURES

1 Jump up to the new signature and enter the first sewing station directly above. Then exit the next sewing station.

2 Grab the thread directly below, but toward the next open sewing station. This is an important concept to keep in mind, because when the next signature is added, the thread is traveling in the opposite direction. Continue in the same way for the other two pairs of sewing stations, then exit the last sewing station.

3 ▼ Tighten the stitching and then proceed with the kettle stitch. A *kettle stitch* is a slipknot used to secure the sewing at the end of each signature. To make the kettle stitch, take the needle and sew in between the two signatures directly below. Leave a small loop, then pass the needle through that loop, pulling up toward the next (new) signature to secure the knot.

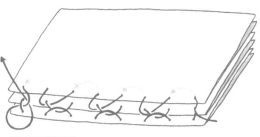

KETTLE STITCH

4 Continue sewing in the same manner for any remaining signatures. Secure with a kettle stitch at the end of each new signature.

5 Finishing with an additional kettle stitch at the end of the last signature is recommended for added security. Trim loose threads to about $1/2$" (1.3 cm).

TIP Sewing onto tapes in conjunction with the link stitch can easily be implemented with this stitch if desired. The tapes provide additional support and the bump created by the tapes creates a more historical look.

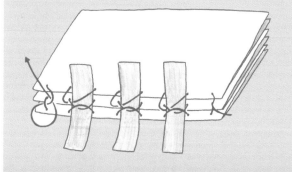

Adding the End Papers

1   Remember to check the paper grain to ensure it is parallel to the spine of the book. Measure and cut two pieces of paper, one each for the front and back of the book. Either a single sheet or folio may be used as an end sheet.

2   Tip on the end sheets with PVA. Carefully glue a ¹⁄₈" (3 mm) adhesive strip along the folded edge of the folio. Place the end sheet onto the text block with the folded edge flush to the spine (see Tipping On and Hinging Panels, page 35).

TIP Before reinforcing the spine with the mull, headbands, and spine liner, the edges may be trimmed on a guillotine for a more professional look. Most copy centers have a guillotine and typically charge by the cut. The book example shown was cut at the head and tail, with a natural foredge. Be careful not to cut into the sewing of the text block.

Reinforcing the Spine

1   The entire process of reinforcing the spine of the text block is covered in the previous Perfect Binding project (see Reinforcing the Spine, page 74).

2   Press the text block and glue the spine with PVA.
▼   Brush the adhesive in between the signatures and over the stitching. Tuck loose threads between the signatures. While the adhesive is wet, the mull can be applied directly to the spine of the text block. The glued spine should dry for several hours.

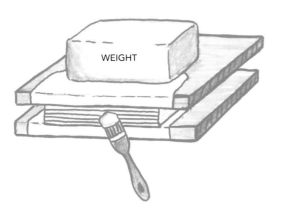
WEIGHT

3   Prepare a piece of mull, bands for the head and
▼   tail if desired, and a spine liner to finish reinforcing the spine.

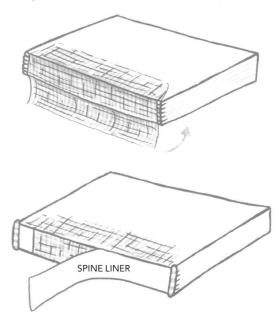
SPINE LINER

Measuring and Constructing the Case

1   Carefully measure the text block again. The average square on a book is approximately ¹⁄₁₆" to ¹⁄₈" (1.6 to 3 mm). A larger square may be needed for larger constructions. Taking the time to cut the cover boards exactly aids in casing in the text block.

2   Mark and cut the height on the board first to ensure that the covers and spine are the same height.

3   Cut two boards to the proper width for the front and back cover.

4   For the spine of the cover, sandwich the text block between the board covers, squeeze tightly, and measure at the spine and foredge. Take the average of these measurements and use this calculation to establish the width of the spine.

Creating an Inset

1 Create an inset on the board before gluing and covering. Since the board is processed in layers it can be carved into to compensate for a paste label. Position the paste label on the board as desired. Measure and draw a line $1/16$" to $1/8$" (1.6 to 3 mm) larger all the way around the label to compensate for the thickness of the covering material.

2 Carefully carve into the board with a craft knife.

▼ Go over each line three to five times. The amount of passes depends on the amount of pressure applied. Do not carve more than halfway through the board because this weakens the cover in that area. Carve down to the thickness of the paste label. *Note:* Straight cuts are easier to carve than curved cuts.

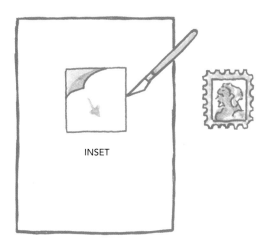

INSET

3 Use the craft knife to lift up one corner and peel off the layers of board as desired. Sometimes the board does not release easily. Peel off the other edges so that it results in a level surface. Once all of the appropriate layers have been peeled away, use the bone folder to burnish the inset smooth.

> **TIP** Stamps, labels, photographs, and decorative papers are just a few of the materials that can be used for insets. The insets can also stand alone to create a unique and subtle design.

Covering the Boards

1 Tape may be used to simulate the joint spacing and test the boards before covering. If any of the calculations are off, recut the boards to the appropriate size. A mixture of two-thirds PVA to one-third methyl cellulose is recommended for covering the board and casing in the text block.

FORMULA FOR THE JOINT SPACER
Joint width = two boards, plus 2 × cloth thickness, plus 1 × square

> **TIP** Instead of using a full piece of cloth to cover the binder's board, a strip of book cloth may be used along the spine edge and part of the cover. Decorative paper would then cover the remaining board. The paper should overlap the cloth to avoid any fraying. Mark the center of the desired cloth width and glue the spine first to ensure an even overlap for each cover. Turn in the edges for the cloth first, then proceed to the paper ends.

2 The Perfect Binding project details the process of covering the boards and casing in the text block (see Perfect Binding—Making the Cover, page 75). The only difference when gluing the boards down to the back side of the book cloth, is to glue the cover with the inset first and place onto the left-hand side of the material. This decreases the chance of forgetting about the inset during covering. Gently use a bone folder to accentuate the recessed areas of the board. Cloth and paper mark up easily with a bone folder, so a clean piece of waste paper should be used to protect the area.

3 Glue the binder's board for the spine and back
▶ cover using the joint spacer provided above
(around $^3/_8$" [1 cm]). Use the cheater's strip to
trim excess cloth around all the edges (see Tools,
page 15). Trim the corners and turn in the edges
before gluing in the text block.

4 Glue the back side of the end sheets and case
▼ in the text block into the cover as demonstrated
with the Perfect Binding project (see Perfect
Binding—Making the Cover, page 75). Remember
not to glue the spine of the cover as this drastically decreases its flexibility. Glue any paste labels
onto the inset area before pressing.

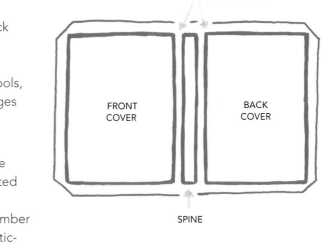

JOINT SPACER

FRONT COVER

BACK COVER

SPINE

5 Look over the book to ensure there is no adhesive
▼ spilling over the edges. If the excess adhesive
has not been removed, the pages may become
fused together while drying. The French groove
reinforces the flexibility of this thicker text block.
Allowing the book to dry overnight under weights
is highly recommended. Do not attempt to open
the book until it is completely dry!

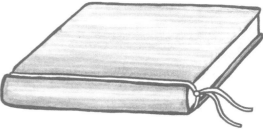

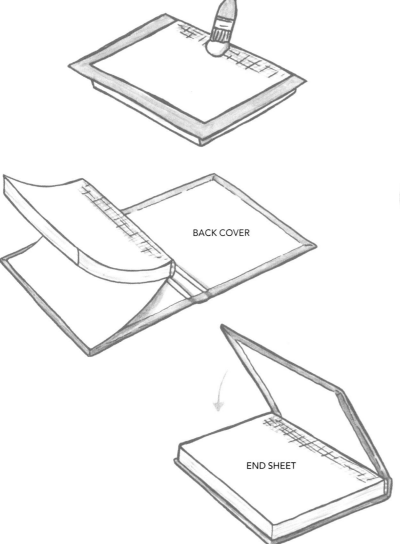

BACK COVER

END SHEET

FORMULA FOR THE MATERIALS

Binder's Board   HEIGHT = height of picture plus 4" (10.2 cm)
                        WIDTH = width of picture plus 4" (10.2 cm)

Center Joint Cloth HEIGHT = 2 boards height, minus 2 × square
                        WIDTH = 2 × turnover plus joint width

Side Joint Cloths   HEIGHT = 2 × turnover plus joint width
                        WIDTH = one board width, minus 2 × square

End Papers   HEIGHT = one board height, minus 2 × square
                        WIDTH = one board width, minus 2 × square

MATERIALS

four 6^1/$_2$" × 8^1/$_2$" (16.5 × 21.6 cm) pieces binder's board for the frame

one 17" × 1^3/$_4$" (43.2 × 4.4 cm) piece of covering material for the center joint cloth

two 1^1/$_2$" × 6^1/$_4$" (3.8 × 15.9 cm) piece of covering material for the side joint cloths

four 8^1/$_4$" × 6^1/$_4$" (21 × 15.9 cm) pieces paper for the end papers

PHOTO FRAME

THIS METHOD OF COVERING BOARD IS USED FOR MULTIPLE-PANEL portfolios. It is slightly altered to house two photos and is meant to stand without a prop on the back. Although book cloth is normally recommended for any joint spacing, decorative paper may be used since the opening and closing of this structure is minimal. This is a great way to accentuate those treasured moments.

Measuring and Constructing the Frame

1   Use a binder's board that is appropriate for the desired frame. Check for grain direction. One of the joints is against the grain when closed. This is unavoidable when using a single covering material for the structure. The grain, however, should be in sync with the covering material to avoid uneven warping.

2   Square the binder's board, and then mark and cut the four boards to the exact size (see Cutting Techniques, page 20).

3   On two pieces, cut a window appropriate for the image that is to be placed inside the frame. *Note:* Undercut ¹/₈" to ¹/₄" (3 to 6 mm) or smaller so that the edges of the photographs are not exposed.

Cutting and Covering Windows

1   When turning in the open windows it is necessary
▼ to cover the inside corners so that the board is not exposed. Cut eight 1" (2.5 cm) squares from the covering material, then fold each piece in half.

2   Glue onto the inside of each corner and allow
▼ to completely dry (edges should hang over on both sides). Once the adhesive has dried, take a straight razor blade or craft knife and trim off the excess material on both sides (this eliminates any bulky corners).

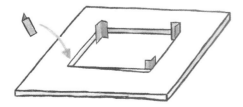

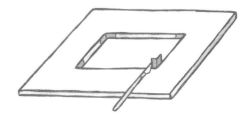

Cutting the Cloth

1 Determine the grain direction of the cloth. Rough-cut the cloth about 2" (5.1 cm) larger in all directions. Cut the cloth to accommodate all four boards, joint spaces, and turn-ins. The general layout is similar to the flat back journal. It is best to use a larger cover material than actually needed.

FORMULA FOR THE JOINT SPACER

Two joint spacers are needed so that the finished frame closes properly. The first joint width is measured for the space between the board with the open window and the solid panel. The second joint width measures between the window-to-window and solid-to-solid panels. This compensates for the thickness of the materials being used. The center joint spacer needs to be larger so that it closes once completed.

First joint width = two boards, plus 2 × cloth thickness, plus 2 × cover papers, plus 1 × photograph

Second joint width = four boards, plus 4 × cloth thickness, plus 4 × cover papers, plus 2 × photograph

Covering the Boards

1 Glue each board with an adhesive mixture of two-thirds PVA to one-third methyl cellulose. The boards may be placed in any order, but it is recommended to glue on the solid board, then the window for each side.

2 Glue the first board (solid panel) on the back side close to one edge of the covering material. Be careful to leave at least ⁵⁄₈" (1.6 cm) extra around the tail and foredge. Flip over and smooth from the other side, making sure that the surface is free of wrinkles and air bubbles.

3 Lay the ruler at the side of the glued board and measure using the formula for the first joint width. Glue one of the window panels directly above the solid panel and smooth.

4 Then lay the ruler at the bottom of the solid panel. Glue and place the second solid panel using the formula for the second joint width and smooth.

5 ▶ Repeat for the second window panel, using the first and second joint widths. When a ruler is placed around the perimeter of the glued boards, all four boards should line up neatly.

6 Use the cheater's strip to trim excess cloth around all edges (see Tools, page 15). Finish the corners as desired and turn-in all four outside edges (see Turning Over the Edges, page 36).

7 ▼ The inside of each window must also be turned in. Start by drawing an X from corner to corner, then trim the edges to the standard turn-in. Glue the turn-ins and turn over each edge individually to the back side of the board. Repeat for the other window.

8 ▼ Cut and glue the longer joint strip to cover the center joint spacing on the back of the boards. The size should be ¹⁄₄" (6 mm) shorter than the height of the finished board height. Center the strip and work into the joint spacing so that it touches the back side of the covering material. Repeat for the smaller joint strips between the solid and window panels in the same manner.

Finishing the Frame

I ▼ Four end sheets are needed to cover the back side of each board. Repeat for the other solid panel. Glue on the first two end sheets to the back side of the solid boards and smooth. The end papers should be at least 1/4" (6 mm) smaller than the actual size of the boards if a 1/8" (3 mm) square is used.

2 Smooth and glue the next end sheet for the window panel. Place a scrap piece of paper underneath the window to avoid a mess with the exposed area. This is removed and trimmed later.

3 Repeat for the other window panel in the same manner. Allow the panels to dry completely under weight for at least one hour before trimming. This prevents the damp covering material from snagging during cutting.

4 ▼ Place the frame faceup and remove the waste paper. Carefully cut along the inside edge of the window to release and reveal the frame for the picture. Cutting from the corner out in all directions yields a cleaner window.

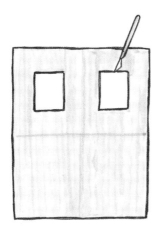

5 ▼ The project is nearly complete. Photo corners may be used on all four edges to secure the photograph onto the inside of the window mat. A piece of acetate or clear Mylar may be placed on top of the photograph for protection.

6 ▼ Hook and loop tape (Velcro) dots may be used to secure the panels. Fold the window frame down and display the double picture frame slightly bent so that it does not fall over.

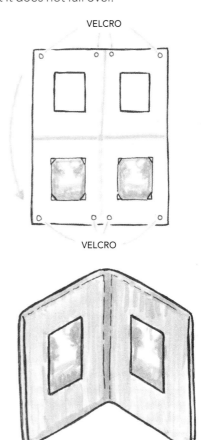

VELCRO

VELCRO

Boxes

3

BUILDING BOXES IS NOT AS DIFFICULT as it might seem; accurate measurements, however, do make construction and covering much easier. This section shows four very distinct boxes; a nonadhesive origami folded box, a simple box with a divider, a triangular box, and a cylindrical box shaped like an antique hatbox. Each of the four boxes has a lid, and the methods shown can easily be adapted to any of the constructions. Complete each project in the order presented to get a better understanding of the basic principles of building in three dimensions. Once again, the formulas are provided as a guide to create customized shapes and sizes.

Some boxes have multiple trays, hinged lids, and complicated closures. As I explored and learned about each of these structures, I found ways of simplifying their construction. The first origami box is composed of three pieces of paper folded individually to make up the various components of the box: the base, the lid, and the divider. The other three boxes (simple, triangular, and cylindrical) deal with covering binder's board from the outside to the inside. The instructions discuss covering the bases and lids with as few pieces of paper as possible to simplify the covering. This creates continuity between surface and form. It is important to keep in mind that with these three bound boxes, the cover material is cut as the box is being covered. Starting with a larger sheet than is actually needed minimizes the need for measuring once the box base is constructed.

Have fun with each structure and, as always, experiment with the materials to create a unique box!

FORMULA FOR THE MATERIALS

Box Base	HEIGHT and WIDTH = 3 × desired finished size
Box Lid	HEIGHT and WIDTH = 3 × the desired finished size (same size as base)
Divider	HEIGHT and WIDTH = $^2/_3$ to $^3/_4$ the size of base paper

MATERIALS

two 8" × 8" (20.3 × 20.3 cm) sheets medium weight paper for the box base and lid

one 5¼" × 5¼" (13.3 × 13.3 cm) sheet light to medium weight paper for the divider

ORIGAMI BOX

with Divider

THIS SIMPLE BOX IS MADE UP OF THREE square pieces of paper. It is a fantastic nonadhesive method for creating a simple and unique gift box. Decorative papers are a great way to enhance the different sections. For smaller boxes, a thinner text-weight paper is recommended. For larger boxes, use a cover stock paper for a more stable structure. Pay close attention to the illustrations to aid in construction.

Making the Base

1 ▶ The paper should be facedown before beginning any folding. Fold the paper in half in one direction and open. Then fold the paper in half in the other direction to make four boxes visually. The intersection of the folds indicates the center of the paper.

2 ▼ Fold each corner to the center point.

3 ▼ Line up one of the outside flat edges with the center mark where all of the points converge. This creates the walls of the box. Repeat for the opposite side.

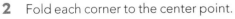

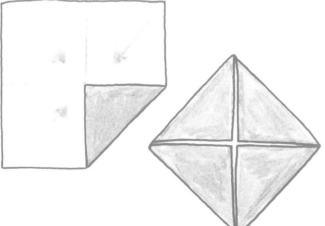

4 Unfold the two sides and repeat the same process
▼ in the other direction for the two remaining sides.

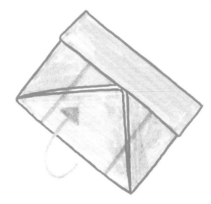

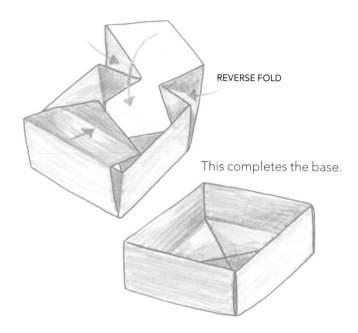

REVERSE FOLD

This completes the base.

5 Open one side of the paper. Then open the
▼ opposite side.

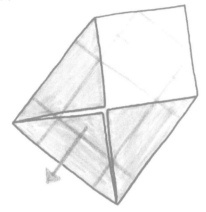

Making the Lid

1 To make the lid, prepare the paper in the same
▼ manner as the base. Stop at the point of building
the walls with the folds (step 3). Instead of lining
up the flat edge to the center point, position the
edge just short of the center, approximately ⅛"
(3 mm) or more depending on the size of the box.
This makes walls that are slightly shorter in height
than the base, and create a larger top surface so
that the two components fit together. Once the
shortened walls are folded, repeat steps 5 and 6
above to complete the lid.

6 Lift the two adjacent folded side walls so that they
▼ are perpendicular to the base. Reverse the folds
in the corners to make the adjacent wall stand up.
This forms two triangles that are tucked underneath the sheet as it is folded over to meet up with
the center point. Repeat the same procedure for
the opposite side.

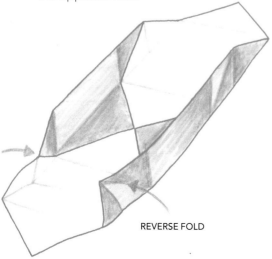

REVERSE FOLD

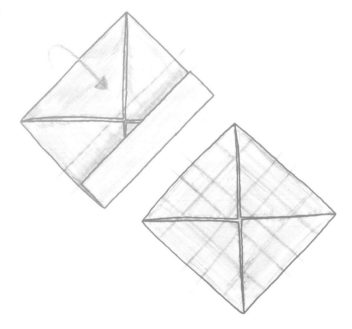

Making the Divider

1 ▶ Position the paper facedown before folding. Fold the square piece of paper diagonally from one corner to the opposite corner. Repeat in the other direction. This is a different way to find the center of the paper.

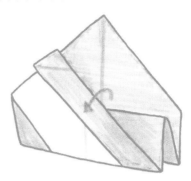

2 ▶ Take one of the corners and align it with the center point. Repeat for the opposite side and stop.

3 ▶ Fold the paper in half so that it creates an upside-down house shape. The face side of the paper should face out.

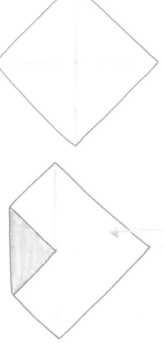

4 ▼ On one half, make the sides line up so the eave of the roof lines up with the top folded edge. Repeat for the eave on the other side of the divider. This creates two folds and forms the divider for the inside of the base.

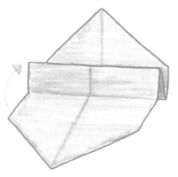

5 ▼ With the pointed ends now faceup, take the right flat edge and turn it down so the bottom right end is parallel to the flat edge at the bottom of the divider. Do the same fold for the left edge on the same side of the divider.

Repeat the same process for the other side of the divider. Folding the edges over makes a smaller square shape, so it fits neatly inside the box base.

6 ▼ Bring the ends down and place the divider into the box base to finish.

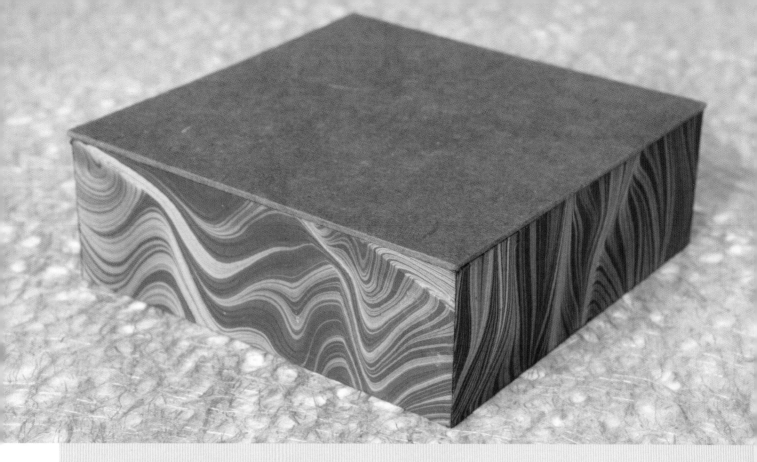

FORMULA FOR THE MATERIALS

Base	HEIGHT = desired size
	WIDTH = desired size
Side Walls (Foredge)	HEIGHT = height of base
	WIDTH = desired wall height
Head and Tail Walls	HEIGHT = width of base, plus 2 × board thickness
	WIDTH = desired wall height
Outer Lid	HEIGHT = base height, plus 2 × board thickness
	WIDTH = base width, plus 2 × board thickness
Inner Lid	HEIGHT = base height, minus 1 board thickness
	WIDTH = base width, minus 1 board thickness
Divider	HEIGHT = wall height, minus 2 × board thickness
	WIDTH = height of base
End Paper	HEIGHT = base height, minus 2 × square
	WIDTH = base width, minus 2 × square

MATERIALS

one 6" × 6" (15.2 × 15.2 cm) piece binder's board for the base

two 6" × 2" (15.2 × 5.1 cm) pieces binder's board for the side walls (foredge)

two 6^1/$_8$" × 2" (15.6 × 5.1 cm) pieces binder's board for the head and tail walls

one 6^1/$_8$" × 6^1/$_8$" (15.6 × 15.6 cm) piece binder's board for the outer lid

one 5^7/$_8$" × 5^7/$_8$" (14.9 × 14.9 cm) piece binder's board for the inner lid

one 6" × 1^{13}/$_{16}$" (15.2 × 4.6 cm) piece binder's board for the divider

two 2^5/$_8$" " × 5^3/$_4$" (6.7 × 14.6 cm) pieces paper for the end papers

SIMPLE BOX
with Divider

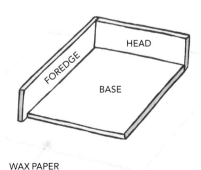

USE THE FORMULA TO CREATE EITHER a rectangular or square box. This is a useful project whether it is meant to hold jewelry or create a slipcase for a bound book. The divider adds a distinctive look and opens the door to many possibilities. Some measuring is needed initially; once the box is assembled, however, covering it with beautiful decorative papers is a snap.

Measuring and Constructing the Box

I
▼ Check for grain direction. Square up the board, then measure and cut the board for the base, walls, and lid (see Determining the Grain, page 18).

2 Cut the boards for the outer and inner lids. The grain direction should be the same as the base of the board for consistency in covering.

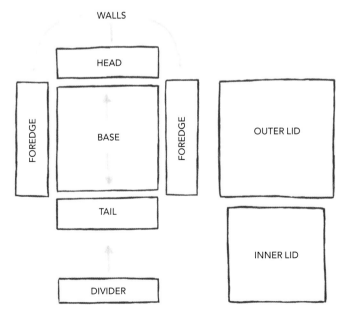

Gluing the Boards

I
▼ Place the base flat on top of a piece of wax paper. Then glue the bottom edge of one side of the box with PVA and place so that it is perpendicular to the table. Make sure it is flush to one edge. Use a weight to stabilize until the other sides are glued.

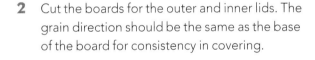

WAX PAPER

2 Next, glue the bottom and side edge nearest the
▼ previously glued board. Check each edge with a
triangle to make sure each wall is 90 degrees from
the table surface. Glue the remaining sides. Press
the walls to the edge of the base to secure. Use
rubber bands around the walls and a weight in the
center to secure the base. *Note:* A small scrap
piece of board may be used to clean up any extra
adhesive on the inside of the box base.

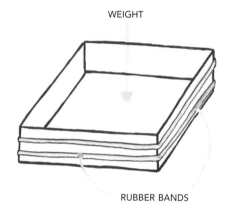

WEIGHT

RUBBER BANDS

3 Allow the base to dry completely. Then sand any
rough or uneven edges. *Note:* The raised edges
show when thinner covering materials are used. It
is best to make sure that the base is smooth and
flat on all sides.

TIP Create a sanding board by gluing a different roughness of sandpaper to each side of a scrap piece of binder's board. This makes a large emery board, which is much easier to use than a loose piece of sandpaper.

Gluing the Divider

1 Cut the divider to the appropriate size and rough-
cut a piece of covering material to encompass
both sides of the divider, plus turn-ins, on both
sides and bottom.

2 Glue one side of the board with a mixture of
▼ two-thirds PVA to one-third methyl cellulose and
place toward the bottom onto the back side of
the material. Glue the other side of the board and
smooth. The material should hang over on the
bottom as well as the ends of the divider.

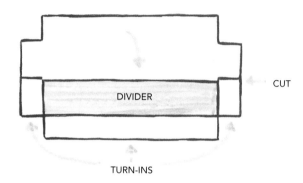

CUT

DIVIDER

TURN-INS

3 Use the cheater's strip and trim a turn-in for the
bottom and sides of the divider.

4 Flip over the divider so the cover edge of the
board is on the table surface. Carefully make a cut
from the board out on both sides to release the
turn-in.

5 Cut straight from the bottom corner of the
▼ binder's board. The trimmed corner should be
a square cut out. It should be cut straight across
to maximize coverage on the inside of the base.
Repeat for the other side.

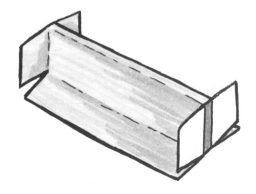

6 Glue the bottom turn-ins individually and position
▼ the divider onto the base. Make sure the divider is
90 degrees to the base and secure the turn-ins to
each wall.

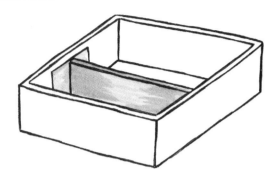

Cutting the Cloth

I Determine the grain direction in the cloth or
paper. Carefully rough-cut the covering material
to encompass the base, outside and inside walls,
and turn-ins. It is best to use a larger covering than
actually needed. As a reminder, the material is
trimmed down as the box is being covered.

Covering the Base

I Glue the base with a mixture of two-thirds PVA
to one-third methyl cellulose, center, and place
onto the back side of the covering material. Flip
over and smooth from the other side, making
sure that it is free of wrinkles and air bubbles.

2 Carefully cut the material so that each side has
▼ enough covering material to stretch from the
outside to the inside with at least a ⅝" (1.6 cm)
turn-in. An additional ⅝" (1.6 cm) turn-in is
needed for the two side panels that are opposite
from one another. Use the cheater's strip to create
turn-ins for the two sides. The other two sides
have a straight cut, covering the turn-ins from
the first two sides.

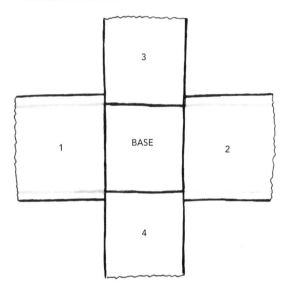

3 Glue one of the walls that have the two turn-ins
and smooth into place. Repeat the same process
for the opposite wall.

4 Cut the turn-ins as they meet up with the lip of
▼ the base to release. Then glue the turn-ins onto
the adjacent sides. Repeat for the other side.

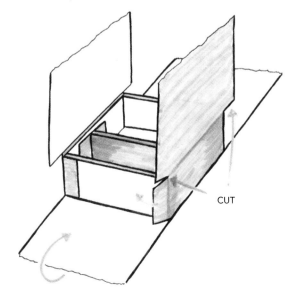

5 Complete the outside covering by gluing the walls that have the secured turn-ins and smooth the material.

6 Lay the box on its side. Each side should be trimmed so that the covering material lines up neatly with the inside corner of the box. Use a triangle to make sure that the cut is perpendicular to the lip of each wall. A small 45-degree angle must be cut to compensate for the thickness of the board at the top lip corners on each wall. Once turned onto the inside, the sides create mitered corners. Repeat for all remaining sides in the same way. There is no overlap on the inside corners of the base walls. The cutting should be exact so the board is not exposed.

7 ▼ Additional cutting is required where the divider meets up with the covering material. Lay the box flat on the side with the divider perpendicular to the table surface. Carefully cut the thickness of the divider on the covering material. Come at least two boards away from the lip to ensure coverage as the material is wrapped to the inside. Initially it is best to cut as little away as possible, and then trim more if necessary. Repeat for the opposite side.

8 Before gluing, fold the material to the inside to ensure a good fit. Crease the material along the inside where the wall meets the base. This should be a very snug fit. Pull the material out, place the cheater's strip along the creased edge, and trim any extra material. Cut the corners of the turn-ins so that they create a mitered corner on the inside bottom of the base.

9 ▼ Carefully glue the material and cover the inside of each wall. To decrease the chance of adhesive sticking to the sides, use wax paper to line the adjacent sides and remove once the materials have been positioned. Use a bone or Teflon folder to ensure crisp inside edges and smooth any wrinkles or air bubbles. Repeat for the other sides. The Teflon folder is ideal because its flat edge makes smoothing the insides of the boxes much easier.

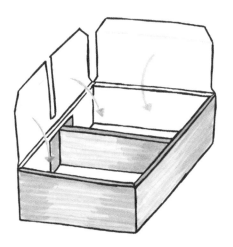

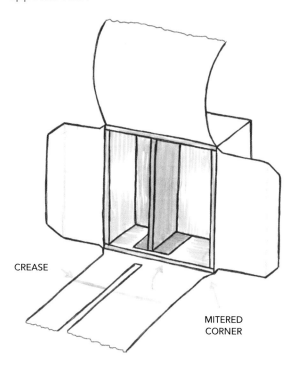

CREASE

MITERED CORNER

Lining the Inside of the Box

1   Measure and cut a piece that is ⅛" (3 mm) shorter on all sides for the inside bottom of the box. Two separate pieces need to be cut for each side of the divider.

2   Glue the back side of one sheet carefully and
▼   position onto the inside of the box. Repeat for the other side of the divider and smooth into place. Use wax paper again to line the walls if necessary.

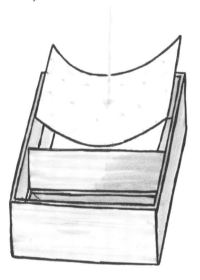

3   Press under weight for one hour to overnight.

Covering the Outer and Inner Lids

1   Glue the outside of the outer lid and smooth. Cut the turn-ins on all sides. Trim the corners and turn in all the sides (see Turning Over the Edges, page 36).

2   Repeat for the inner lid in the same manner.

3   Glue the back side of the inner lid and center onto
▼   the back side of the outer lid. Press under weight until completely dry.

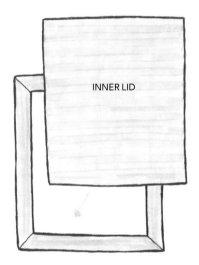

INNER LID

TIP   A multitude of closures and fasteners may be created to keep the box closed. Snaps, hook and loop tape (Velcro), strings, and bone clasps may be used. Personal aesthetics and the materials may dictate the appropriate method.

FORMULA FOR THE MATERIALS

Bottom Base	= desired size, cut to 60 degrees at each point
Wall or Sides of Box	= width of base side plus 2 × board thickness
Outer Lid	= size of constructed box (base plus 1 board thickness) on all edges or about 2 boards larger in height and width
Inner Lid	= size of base, minus 1 board thickness
Ribbon	= desired loop size plus 2" (5.1 cm)

MATERIALS

one 6 1/8" (15.6 cm) -tall triangle of binder's board, measuring from the flat edge to the point for the base

three 3" × 7 1/4" (7.6 × 18.4 cm) pieces binder's board for the walls or sides

one 6 1/4" (15.9 cm) triangle binder's board, measuring from the flat edge to the point for the outer lid

one 6" (15.2 cm) triangle binder's board, measuring from the flat edge to the point for the inner lid

one 7" (17.8 cm) length ribbon or leather cording for the loop on the outer lid

TRIANGULAR BOX

Geometry of Triangles

TRIANGLES HAVE THREE POINTS ALL WITH DIFFERENT angles. For any triangle, when the three angles are added together, they total 180 degrees. Triangle tools, available at art supply stores, come with either 45/45/90-degree angles or 30/60/90-degree angles. Both types are helpful when constructing books and boxes. For this box a 30/60/90-degree triangle is necessary to achieve the correct angles. An equilateral triangle is composed of three angles, each having 60 degrees.

It is recommended to begin with the Simple Box with Divider (see page 94) to familiarize yourself with basic procedures if this is the first attempt at making a box. The covering methods are similar, but the sharper angles may present a challenge initially.

Measuring and Constructing the Box

1 Check for grain direction. Square the board, and then mark and cut a strip of board the total height of the base. The height is measured from the flat edge to the point. Cutting the board in this manner makes multiples very easy.

2 ▼ Use the 60-degree angle so that it rests along one edge and cut.

3 ▶ Flip the triangle horizontally so that the angle faces the opposite direction. Carefully line up with the flat edge to the point of the newly cut angle. Mark and cut to make an equilateral triangle.

4 Cut a strip to the height of the sides, ensuring that the grain runs perpendicular to the base. Cutting shorter walls is recommended (3" [7.6 cm] or less) to make construction easier. Then cut the width for each board. A total of three boards cut to the exact same size are needed for the triangular box.

5 Measure and cut the boards for the outer and inner lid to the exact same shape of the base. The grain direction should be the same as the base of the board and the covering material. Both boards are cut in the same manner as the base, just at varying sizes.

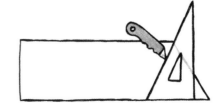

Beveling the Edges

I ▼ Use sandpaper to create a 30-degree angle at the edges of the walls. Bevel the edges on the same side of the board, so that when the walls are glued together they form a neat mitered corner. Repeat for the other two walls.

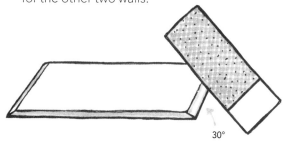

30°

Gluing the Boards

I ▼ Place the base on a piece of wax paper so that it is flat on the table surface. Use PVA to glue the bottom edge of one side of the wall and place next to the base. Center and make sure it is perpendicular to the table. Use a weight to stabilize until the next side is glued.

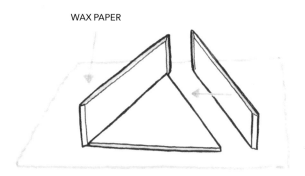

WAX PAPER

2 Glue along the bottom and side of the adjacent edge, and press into place. Glue the last side the same way, adding PVA to the bottom and both beveled edges, and secure into place. Check the wall with a triangle to make they are square to the table surface.

3 Place rubber bands on the outside and weights inside so that the boards maintain their shape. Allow to dry completely so that the boards do not move. Remember to check that all angles are 60 degrees. Once the box is dry, sand as necessary to smooth any uneven edges.

Cutting the Cloth

I Determine the grain direction in the cloth or paper. The grain is a little awry with this structure since there are an odd number of sides. As a starting point, the grain should run parallel to the box base. To avoid this problem, choose a paper that does not have a grain. This decreases the chance of unexpected warping.

2 Carefully place the box base and rough-cut cloth or paper about two times larger in all directions. The cloth or paper is trimmed down after the base has been glued to the back side of the covering material. The paper or cloth should be large enough to cover the base, outside walls, inside walls, and turn-ins on the inside of the base.

Covering the Boards

I Center and glue the bottom of the base with an adhesive mixture (two-thirds PVA to one-third methyl cellulose) and place onto the back side of the material. Flip over and smooth from the other side, making sure that it is free of wrinkles and air bubbles.

2 Rough-cut the material so each side has enough material to stretch from the outside to the inside with at least a ⅝" (1.6 cm) turn-in. An additional ⅝" (1.6 cm) turn-in is added to two sides before gluing.

3 ▼ One side has two turn-ins, and the adjacent side has one turn-in nearest the third and final side, which has no turn-ins. See the diagram for the proper layout. Use a triangle and the cheater's strip for the square cuts and turn-ins on the sides. This covering method is similar to the Simple Box with Divider project (see page 94).

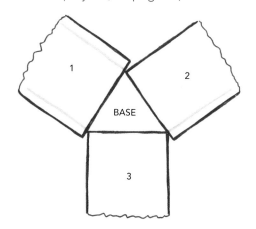

1   2   BASE   3

4 Glue the wall of the first side that has the two
▼ turn-ins and smooth. Lay the box flat on its side and trim from the edge of the board on each end to release each turn-in. Then glue the turn-ins onto the adjacent sides. Repeat the same process for the second wall. Continue in the same way for the third and final wall. The last wall covers the turn-ins to make a neat edge.

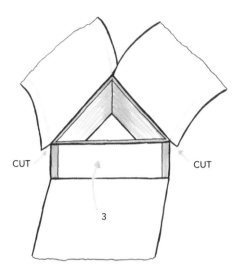

CUT   CUT

3

5 Each side should be trimmed so that the covering material lines up neatly to the inside corner of the box. Use a triangle to make sure that the cut is perpendicular to the flat edge of the wall. A small angle of 30 to 45 degrees must be cut to compensate for the thickness of the board at the top lip corners on each wall. Once turned over, the sides create mitered corners. Repeat for all remaining sides in the same way.

6 Before gluing, fold the material to the inside
▼ to ensure a good fit. Crease the material along the inside where the wall meets the base. This should be a snug fit with precise cutting. Pull the material out and place the cheater's strip along the creased edge and trim any extra material. Cut the corners of the turn-ins at a 30- to 45-degree angle to create a mitered corner for the inside of the base.

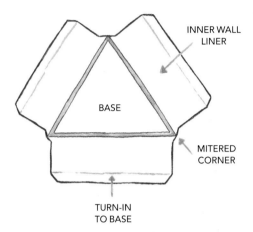

INNER WALL
LINER

BASE

MITERED
CORNER

TURN-IN
TO BASE

7 Carefully glue the material and cover the inside of each wall. To decrease the chance of adhesive sticking to the adjacent sides, use wax paper to line the side and remove once the material has been positioned. Use a bone or Teflon folder to ensure crisp inside edges and smooth any wrinkles and air bubbles.

Lining the Inside of the Box

1 Measure and cut a piece of material that is ⅛" (3 mm) shorter on all three edges to cover the inside of the base. This serves as the end paper.

2 Line the sides with wax paper and remove once the end paper is positioned to prevent adhesives from staining the walls during placement. Glue the end paper on the back side, and then center and lay it down onto the inside of the box base. Smooth any air bubbles or wrinkles.

Creating the Box Lid

1 Glue the outer lid and smooth. Use the cheater's strip and trim the turn-ins on all three sides.

2 ▼ Cut the corners a board's thickness away from each point. Each corner should be at a 30-degree angle instead of the 45-degree angle, which is typically used on square corners. Trim each corner in the same way.

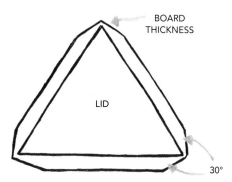

3 Glue and turn over each side. It is important to remember to pinch each overhang toward the adjacent side to minimize an excessively pointed corner. Repeat for the other two sides (see Triangle Accordion, page 64).

4 Cover the inner lid in the same way. Proceed to the next step before gluing the outer and inner lids together.

Creating the Loop Handle

1 ▼ Chisel or cut a slit in the center of the outer lid appropriate to the width of the ribbon. Work on top of a punching board to protect the working surface.

2 Open the slit as necessary to feed the ribbon through to the back side of the outer lid. A butter knife or micro-spatula may be used to stretch open the hole, making it easier to feed the ribbon through to the other side.

3 ▼ Feed the loose ends of the ribbon to the back side of the outer lid.

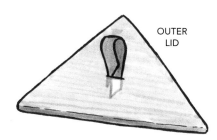

4 Cut a channel or inset for each end of the ribbon on the back side to minimize the bulk of the ribbon when glued (see Creating an Inset, page 82). Secure to the inside of the lid by gluing each end of the loose ribbon. Use a hammer to flatten the ribbons. This also closes the chiseled slit to secure the ribbon even more.

5 ▼ Finish the cover by gluing the back side of the inner lid. Center the glued lid to the underneath side of the outer lid giving equal spacing on all three sides.

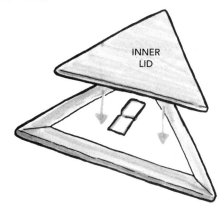

6 Lay the ribbon flat so that it creases evenly on both sides and press under weights to ensure a tight bond.

ROUND BOX

(Cylindrical)

Dimensions
19" (circumference) × 4¹/₁₆"
(48.3 [circumference] × 10.3 cm)

THIS WONDERFUL BOX IS REMINISCENT OF THE
old style hatboxes. What a satisfying shape to hold
treasured items, a stamp collection, shells, or jewelry.
Although the covering style is similar to the simple
and triangular boxes, there are a few additional secrets
to getting a smooth and uniform cylindrical shape.
This is perhaps one of the most challenging projects
because it forces the bookbinder to work in the round
instead of with flat surfaces. This is a favorite among
many book-arts students. Enjoy!

Measuring and Constructing the Box

1 See formula for the materials, page 106. Check
   for the grain direction so that the wall grain runs
   perpendicular to the base. This ensures greater
   stability for the box.

2 With a compass, draw a circle on a piece of a
   board to the exact circumference of the form.
   Carefully cut the base with a heavy utility knife or
   circular mat cutter. Sand the edges so the base is
   the same shape as the form.

3 ▶ Measure and cut a strip of
   board to the desired height;
   3" (7.6 cm) or less is recommended the first time for
   easier construction. Then
   measure the perimeter of
   the form. The overall width
   should measure the entire
   perimeter of the base plus
   ³/₄" (1.9 cm).

FORM

4 ▼ Cut a channel or inset at one end of the board
   and repeat for the opposite end on the other side
   to ensure that the ends meet when glued. This
   also helps to decrease an excessively bulky wall.

INSET

INSET

5 Measure and cut the board for the lid in the same
   way. Allow at least ¹/₂" to 1" (1.3 to 2.5 cm) extra
   for the circumference depending on the cover
   materials used. Cut a channel at each end in the
   same way as the base wall. A heavy piece of paper
   or thin board should be used to compensate
   for the covering material before wrapping the
   boards around the form.

FORMULA FOR THE MATERIALS

Cylindrical Form	HEIGHT and WIDTH = larger than desired size box size (perfect cylinder)
Bottom Base	HEIGHT and WIDTH = desired size, cut to a perfect circle; circumference of form
Base Walls	HEIGHT = desired finished height WIDTH = circumference of base, plus ¾" (1.9 cm)
Lid Base	HEIGHT and WIDTH = circumference of constructed box (base plus 2 × board thickness)
Lid Walls	HEIGHT = desired height, not to exceed height of walls for base WIDTH = circumference of base, plus ¾" (1.9 cm), plus liner
Cushion for Walls	HEIGHT = larger than wall height for lid WIDTH = circumference of base, minus ½" (1.3 cm)

MATERIALS

one 16½" (41.9 cm) -diameter cardboard tube for the cylindrical form

one 5¼" (13.3 cm) -diameter piece binder's board for the bottom base

one 18" × 4" (45.7 × 10.2 cm) piece binder's board for the base wall

one 5⅝" (14.3 cm) -diameter piece binder's board for the lid base

one 19¾" × 2" (50.2 × 5.1 cm) piece binder's board for the lid wall

one 17½" (44.5 cm) piece heavy weight paper or thin board for the cushion between the walls

Forming the Walls

1 Line the form with a layer of wax paper to protect the surface, and secure with tape. This keeps the form from warping or becoming damaged due to the moisture from the dampened boards.

2 Dampen the boards with a sponge and water on both sides to soften. Gently curve the board to fit around the form. Place a heavy paper as a cushion before dampening the wall strip for the lid. Rubber bands may be placed around the form to secure the shape while wrapping the entire form with an elastic wrap bandage. The order of the boards should be the base wall, the liner, and then the lid wall.

3 With a light piece of board as a cushion on top of the base wall strip, place the wall strip for ▼ the lid directly on top of the cushion. Use the rubber bands to encompass all three layers and temporarily secure.

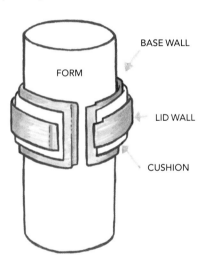

BASE WALL

FORM

LID WALL

CUSHION

4 Tightly wrap the walls with an elastic bandage. An elastic bandage is recommended instead of rubber bands for better and more even pressure. Allow the boards to dry thoroughly before gluing to the base. Letting the boards dry naturally on a form ensures an even cylindrical shape. A fan or hair dryer may be used to speed up the process, but try not to rush. Letting the project sit overnight is recommended.

Gluing the Boards Together

1 Once the warped walls are dry, remove the elastic bandage and/or rubber bands. Discard the heavy paper cushion and save the walls for both the base and lid.

2 Glue one of the channeled edges and join the tabs together to form the cylinder. Pinch tightly until dry or use clamps to secure. The walls should be glued together before gluing the bases inside.

3 Test the base before gluing. If the board bows or ▼ falls out too easily, sand or cut another piece to the appropriate size. Place the wall on a piece of wax paper so that it sits flat on the table surface, then put a line of glue on the inside bottom edge of the walls. Gently push the base to the bottom of the wall. The fit should be snug.

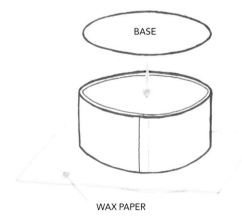

BASE

WAX PAPER

4 Before gluing, check the fit on the lid wall. It should be about ¹/₈" (3 mm) larger around the entire perimeter. This space tightens once covered. Trim the inset end tabs to shorten the circumference if necessary. Repeat the above process to secure the lid wall to the circular base.

5 Allow the boards to dry completely. Sand the base and lid to eliminate any rough or raised edges, especially where the boards are joined together for the walls.

Cutting the Covering Material

I Determine the grain direction in the cloth or paper. The grain should run parallel to the walls. Square the covering material and cut to the height of the walls plus two turn-ins ($^5/_8$" [1.6 cm] each) for the head and tail (see Turning Over the Edges, page 36).

2 Take the same piece of covering material and cut the length so it is long enough to accommodate the perimeter of the wall plus $^5/_8$" (1.6 cm) overlap.

Covering the Outside Boards

I Glue the outside of the box walls with a mixture of two-thirds PVA to one-third methyl cellulose, making sure there is an even $^5/_8$" (1.6 cm) overhang at the base and lip of the wall. Glue the overlap and secure into place.

2 For covering the bottom of the base, cut notches
▼ (darts) in $^1/_2$" (1.3 cm) intervals all along the edge. Cut each notch at a slight angle to minimize any overlapping. The width of the dart depends on the size of the box. The larger the box or circular shape, the narrower the dart should be.

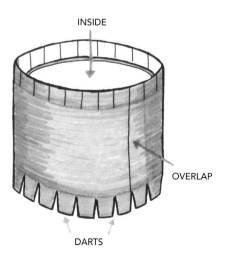

INSIDE

OVERLAP

DARTS

3 Glue each tab and turn-in to the bottom of the base.

4 Cut tabs at $^1/_2$" (1.3 cm) intervals for the lip of the
▼ wall. Do not cut angles for this side or else the board will be exposed once the tabs are turned-in. Glue and turn in each tab.

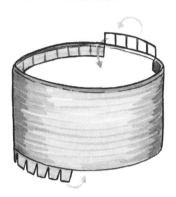

5 For the bottom of the box, cut a liner piece measured to fit inside the darted edges to compensate for the thickness of the turn-ins. Glue and smooth into place.

6 Then cover the bottom with a piece of material
▼ slightly smaller than the circumference of the base, about $^1/_{16}$" (1.6 mm) smaller. Glue and smooth into place.

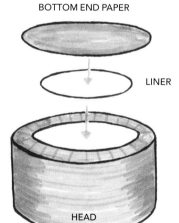

BOTTOM END PAPER

LINER

HEAD

Covering the Inside

1 For the inside wall of the box, cut a strip that is the height of the wall plus ½" (1.2 cm). The length should be the internal circumference plus ⅝" (1.6 cm). Use the cheater's strip to score and fold along the length of the covering material. Make darted tabs along the bottom of the turn-in strip ½" (1.3 cm) apart. These notches should be cut at a slight angle in the same way as the bottom of the base to minimize overlapping. *Note:* The inside lining rests a little below the lip of the wall, similar to an end paper.

2 ▼ To finish the inside, glue the back side of the material, but not the tabs. Carefully place inside the box. To make securing the material easier, line up one end first, then spiral the material down until the other end overlaps the starting point and smooth into place. This is a bit cumbersome at first.

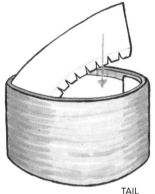

TAIL

3 ▼ Glue each tab and secure to the base.

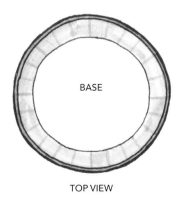

BASE

TOP VIEW

4 ▼ Cut an inside base circle ¼" (6 mm) smaller in diameter. This serves as an end paper for the inside of the box. If desired a liner piece may be added before gluing down the end paper piece. Glue the back side of the end paper, smooth, and secure into place.

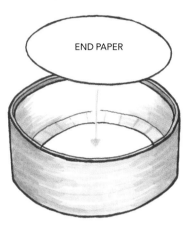

END PAPER

5 ▼ Repeat all of the previous steps in the same way to complete the top lid. Before covering the lid, double-check that the lid fits comfortably on top of the base. Heavier materials may add considerable bulk and the opposite is true for thinner papers. Remember, the shape may be adjusted for the lid wall by cutting small amounts off of the end of the board where it overlaps.

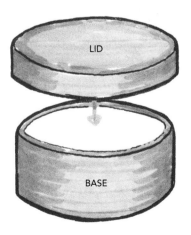

LID

BASE

Surface Design Techniques

4

ALL OF THE TECHNIQUES SHOWN IN this section are ideal for use in any of the book or box projects previously demonstrated. Explore the various processes to add a personalized touch to your materials and projects. By trying the various surface design techniques, the possibilities for application and visual appeal are endless.

The topics covered in this section include making rubber stamps, paste papers, photocopy transfers, and paper dyeing. The setup is minimal and no special equipment is needed, just a little space to work. Page through the Gallery of Artist's Books section (page 125) to see how other artists have used some of the following methods.

FORMULA FOR THE MATERIALS

White Plastic Eraser   HEIGHT and WIDTH = desired stamp size

Ink Pad   HEIGHT and WIDTH = large enough to encompass stamp

MATERIALS

one 2¹⁄₂" × ³⁄₄" (6.4 × 1.9 cm) plastic eraser cut in half for the stamp

several 2¹⁄₂" × 4" (6.4 × 10.2 cm) or larger ink pads in different colors for stamping

TIP Larger sheets of rubber material may be found in most major art supply stores, but are more expensive. The surface is much larger and you will need cutting tools made for linoleum cutting. A less expensive alternative is dense craft foam, which may be cut with scissors and applied to a wooden block for stability.

Drawing and Cutting the Stamp

1. Stamping is a relief form of printing, so whatever is on the highest surface prints. Keep in mind that anything that is drawn is *not* going to be cut away. It is important to remember that the image prints in reverse, so if text is used, it must be drawn on backwards to appear lright side up once stamped. A simple, clean drawing with heavier edges is easier and more legible when cutting and stamping. Clearly draw the symbol onto one surface of the white plastic eraser.

RUBBER STAMPING

RUBBER STAMPS ARE A GREAT WAY TO CREATE A UNIQUE, personal, and cryptic language. Symbols may be used instead of text to build up the surface of the material or stand alone as an icon. The process of making the individual stamps is quite easy. A white plastic eraser, a craft knife, a marker or pencil, and an ink pad are all that is needed. This type of eraser is great to work with because it cuts like butter and is very easy to find in art and craft stores.

2 ▶ Carefully use the craft knife to outline the drawing on the eraser. Take the craft knife at an angle and cut outside of the printing area to release the unwanted material. Repeat on all edges to reveal the printing surface. Linoleum cutting tools may also be used to remove any material from the surface of the eraser.

TIP Ink pads come in a wide variety of colors, but sometimes the size can be restrictive. To make a reusable pad, cut a piece of felt to the desired size and place into a flat tray. A casserole dish works well. Mix the color as desired with water-based pigments and saturate the surface. Stamp as desired, then wash the felt with water to reuse on future projects.

3 ▼ Test the stamp periodically on a scrap piece of paper. Push the stamp on top of the wet ink surface of the ink pad, then press firmly onto the paper to reveal the symbol or image. Cut away any other unwanted printing areas and repeat the process of testing the stamp until satisfied with the results.

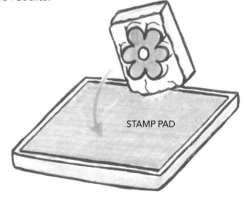

STAMP PAD

4 Once the stamp is complete, use the stamp to decorate the surface of the paper as desired. Multiple stamps can be used to create patterns or overlap one another to reveal a rich and dense surface. Be creative and have fun with it!

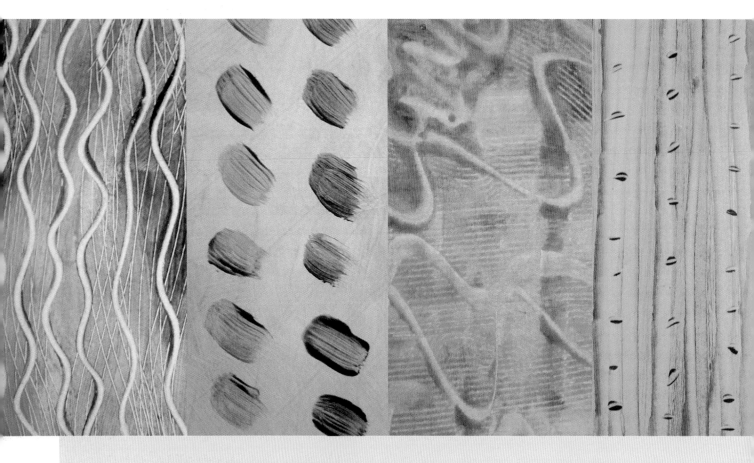

FORMULA FOR THE MATERIALS

Paper	HEIGHT and WIDTH = desired paper size
Plexiglas	HEIGHT and WIDTH = large enough to accommodate paper

MATERIALS

ten or more 8" × 10" (20.3 × 25.4 cm) sheets lightweight paper for the paste paper

one 10" × 12" (25.4 × 30.5 cm) piece Plexiglas as a working surface for the paste paper

TOOLS

Combs

Paintbrushes

Sponges

Stamps

PASTE PAPER RECIPE (by Bonnie Stahlecker)

1 ³/₄ cups (414 ml) distilled water

¹/₄ cup (40 to 50 g) wheat starch, rice starch, rice flour, or white cake flower (Soft as Silk)

glycerin

Ivory soap (powdered)

PASTE PAPERS

ANY PASTE RECIPE MAY BE USED FOR PASTE PAPERS, even methyl cellulose. The paste is not meant to stand alone, so it is recommended to add a little acrylic gel medium as a sealant. Depending on the pigments used, this may not be necessary. Acrylic paints have a gel medium base and automatically add a protective layer. Bonnie Stahlecker created the paste paper recipe demonstrated here. Experiment with other recipes and compare your results (see Recipes, page 32). Additional examples of paste papers are at the end of this section (see Gallery of Artist's Books, page 125).

Making the Paste

1   Preheat 1¹/₂ cups (354.9 ml) of water in a saucepan or microwave.

2   Mix ¹/₄ cup (59.1 ml) of cold water with ¹/₄ cup (40 to 50 g) of the desired flour in a small bowl and whisk until smooth.

3   Pour the flour mixture into the top pot of a double boiler. Once the mixture boils, add the 1¹/₂ cups (354.9 ml) of heated water. Add all at once to prevent any lumps from forming.

4   Continue to heat the paste in a double boiler, stirring constantly. After five to seven minutes, the paste turns from an opaque white to a slightly translucent color. The longer the paste cooks, the thicker it becomes.

5   Remove from the heat and continue to stir until it is lukewarm. Add a few drops of glycerin and soap to the paste. If lumps appear and do not smooth out again, strain the paste through a sieve and discard the lumps. To extend the life of the paste, add a few drops of wintergreen or clove oil. These oils retard the fermentation process and may add a few extra days of usability to the paste.

TIP Remember that pastes last three to four days at room temperature or several weeks when refrigerated. The mixture may need to be reheated slightly once refrigerated. Adding a small amount of water may also be required if the paste is too thick to spread evenly.

Preparing to Work

Choice of pigments: acrylic, tempera, watercolor, or gouache paint

1 ▼ Spoon the paste equally into smaller containers, and mix with the desired pigments. The recommended ratio is ½ cup (118.3 ml) paste to 2 tablespoons (29.6 ml) liquid pigment. Decide the color palette ahead of time so that there is enough paste to work with. The amount of pigment can vary: the more pigment used, the more opaque the color of the paste. The color mixes best when the paste is still warm.

2 ▼ Set up a workstation and protect any surfaces with a plastic tablecloth. This makes for easier cleanup. A clean tray filled with water may be used to wet the paper before creating the paste paper designs. A large rectangular casserole dish works very well. A bowl for cleaning out the tools and sponge is also handy to have around. A brush for each colored paste is suggested to minimize contaminating the colors. Sponges, combs, pastels, chalk, stamps, and any other marking tools may be used to create patterns.

COMBS

STAMPS

SPONGE

FABRIC

3 ▼ Dip the paper in the water and drip off any excess water. This makes the paper adhere to the Plexiglas work surface. Apply the colored paste to the dampened paper and begin working on the designs and patterns.

TIP Combs can be made out of scrap pieces of cardboard and cut into any pattern that is desired. Comb tools are a great way to customize a design.

DAMP PAPER

4 Drag the combs across the surface in different directions to create a pattern. Also consider alternative tools and stamps to create an interesting design. Remove the finished paste paper carefully, and place onto a scrap piece of paper or blotter to dry. Check after one hour to make sure no paper is sticking to the drying surface.

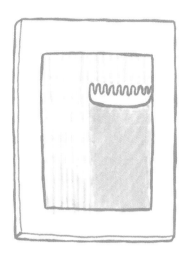

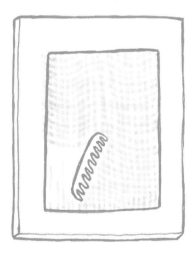

5 Repeat the process by changing the tools around to create unique patterns. If the pattern started does not turn out as intended, simply wipe off or apply more paste and try a new design. The paste papers are very forgiving and versatile while the paste is still wet. Once the paper is dry it may be dampened to apply a second layer of pattern or color. The other side may be used to create a two-sided paste paper. Some thin handmade papers automatically create a double-sided paste paper after the paste is applied and has had a chance to dry.

6 Clean all of the tools and working surfaces with water. A little soap may be used to clean off any dried paste.

7 After the paste papers are completely dry, they may need to be stacked and pressed to flatten the surface. If the paper is applied with an adhesive to the cover board, then no pressing is required. The moisture from the paste softens the paper and should flatten any warping or buckles. A spray water bottle may be used to mist the back before pressing to assist in flattening the paper.

FORMULA FOR THE MATERIALS

Photocopy   HEIGHT and WIDTH = desired image size

MATERIALS

Several photocopies of the same image are suggested as a backup. The density of the image may significantly affect how the image transfers. The more contrast in the image, the more distinctive the transfer. Color photocopies can be more difficult if transferred by hand, because they have four layers of toner compared to the black-and-white copy, which only has one layer.

PHOTOCOPY TRANSFERS

BELIEVE IT OR NOT, A COLOR OR BLACK-AND-WHITE photocopy may be transferred to almost any surface. There are several ways in which the copy may be transferred. The basic idea is that a solution is used to reliquify the toner, causing the toner to transfer onto another surface once pressure is applied. *(Note:* Laser and ink-jet printouts typically do not work when transferring an image with the processes described below. Sometimes you can have success with ink-jet printouts using water as a releasing agent if the original print out is on very glossy paper that has not absorbed the ink.)

NONTOXIC PRODUCTS FOR TRANSFERS

Most schools and artists are using nontoxic methods for transferring an image. The following chemicals may be used and do not require any special ventilation. Many people have allergies, and it is best to test any new product in an open area or outside to decrease the chance of irritation.

WINTERGREEN OIL: A fresh and minty-smelling solution. It is typically diluted in water and used as a liniment to relieve aches and pains. However, it does contain an aspirin derivative, methyl salicylate. If the user is pregnant, do not use! The oil, although natural, can have adverse effects on the unborn fetus. The transfer result is relatively clear, but some stringing of the toner may occur. The paper surface could appear stained for several days until the oil has had a chance to evaporate. The product may be found behind the counter at most pharmacies, but it does not require a prescription.

CITRUS-BASED SOLVENT: This cleaning solvent works well when transferring and is also great for larger surface areas. Although it is not completely nontoxic it yields a clean transfer. Some staining may occur, but it should evaporate in a day or two. This is typically found at hardware stores.

NATURAL ENVIRONMENTAL CLEANING AGENTS: These cleaning solvents are also less offensive in odor and chemical makeup compared to the other solvents. Although similar to the citrus-based solvents, not all of them work, so test before using them on a project. They can be found at most grocery and hardware stores.

CLEAR BLENDER MARKER: The marker has a lacquer-based solvent, but in a much smaller quantity compared to buying a whole can. Essentially it is a marker without any pigment. It is used in illustration to blend several colors together and may be found at most major art supply stores. The marker tends to run out quickly and if not capped properly, dries out. Many artists prefer this pen because it is portable and allows more control in the application. This marker is not recommended for transferring large image areas. There are a number of manufacturers that make this type of marker.

Transferring the Image

SOLVENT PRODUCTS FOR TRANSFERS

The more toxic methods of transferring an image are far more reliable, but the solvents used have a strong odor and cause a slight cooling effect when they come in contact with the skin. The problem with using solvents like these is that they soak directly into the central nervous system. Over a long period of time this may cause numbness to the extremities and damage the liver or kidneys. Both acetone and lacquer thinner evaporate quickly and proper ventilation is required when working with them indoors. The benefit is that there is no staining and most of the toner from the photocopy transfers, yielding much better results.

ACETONE: This solvent has the strongest odor; a respirator with filters that block out organic vapors should be worn with goggles and heavy rubber gloves. Many fingernail polish removers contain an acetone derivative to strip off the enamel coloring though several companies have removed the solvent, opting for a more physically and environmental friendly alternative. This solvent is found in hardware stores.

LACQUER THINNER: Similar to acetone, this solvent should be used in the same way in terms of preparation and protection. This may also be found in a hardware or major art supply store.

1 Make extra copies of each image from a photocopy machine. A fresh photocopy works the best to ensure a more reliable transfer.

2 ▼ Lay the image to be transferred facedown onto the desired surface. Tape may be used on the outside of the image area to prevent slipping; the solvent, however, will not penetrate the surface of the tape. Avoid covering any of the image areas by taping along the outside border.

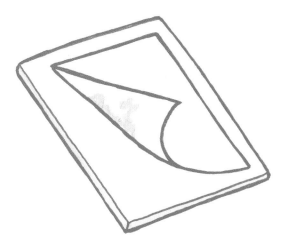

3 ▼ Douse a paper towel with the solvent and rub over the back of the photocopy until the image appears through the paper. If using acetone or lacquer thinner, use a brush to apply the solvent to the back side of the photocopy. This is necessary because the solvent evaporates quickly.

Transferring the Image With a Press

4 Place a few protective sheets of waste paper over
▼ the top and use a spoon to burnish the back side of the photocopy to transfer the image. Carefully lift up the corner of the image to make sure all areas have been transferred. If the transfer is not complete, rewet any dry areas of the photocopy and continue burnishing with the spoon.

1 When using a press for transfers, set the pressure on the press for the materials being used; three pieces of newsprint and a sheet of heavy cardboard provide a firm surface for the transfer.

2 Apply the solvent in the same manner as demonstrated before. Add a few extra sheets of newsprint and a piece of cardboard over the top and run through the press.

3 Peel up a corner of the image to see if it transferred. Rewet as needed and run through the press again. Additional pressure may be required if the image does not transfer after several runs through the press.

4 When using acetone or lacquer thinner, liberally saturate a sheet of heavy weight paper with the solvent. Then lay the saturated sheet directly over the back side of the image area. This decreases the chance of oversaturating the photocopy and pooling the toner. Pooling can cause the image to streak, losing detail and creating a less predictable transfer. This process must be done quickly to avoid losing any of the transferred images due to evaporation.

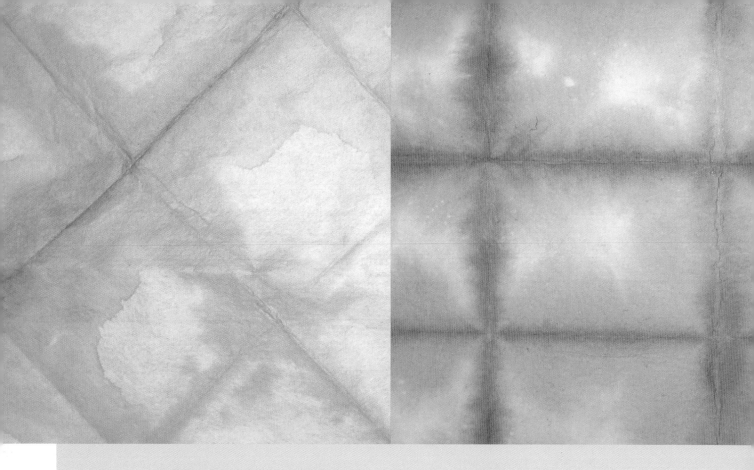

FORMULA FOR THE MATERIALS

Paper   HEIGHT and WIDTH = desired finished paper size

MATERIALS

several 8" × 10" (20.3 × 25.4 cm) pieces handmade or lightweight paper for dyeing

Folding the Paper

1 Fold the paper in an eight-panel accordion for
▶ a symmetrical design (see Accordion with Woven Panels, page 55).

2 Then fold the paper back and forth in any pattern.
▶ Starting at one corner and folding over to meet the folded edge yields a triangular shape. Try several different ways of folding the paper to determine which patterns work best. Simply crinkling the paper up can also create very interesting effects.

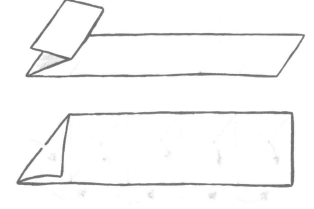

ORIZOMI GOMI

(Paper Dyeing)

THE ART OF PAPER DYEING IS A WONDERFUL WAY TO BREAK up the surface of the paper. *Orizomi Gomi* or *Itajme* is the Japanese term for dyeing paper. The method demonstrated is similar to tie-dyeing T-shirts, so the possibilities are endless. An absorbent paper is necessary for dyeing; many heavy papers need to be pre-soaked for at least four hours in a tray of water. Use a permanent dye such as liquid watercolors, food coloring, acrylic paint, permanent heavy dyes, tempera paint, or calligraphy ink. Protect your work area with a plastic tablecloth and wear protective gloves to avoid staining.

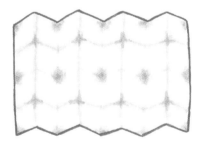

Dyeing the Paper

1 Protect the work area with a plastic tablecloth or scrap paper. Fill several bowls or jars with some water. Make sure that the opening is large enough to accommodate the folded paper.

2 ▼ Place four to eight drops of pigment into ¹⁄₄ cup (59.1 ml) of water and mix thoroughly. The ratio between the amount of water and pigment determines the intensity of the color. The less water used, the more vibrant the color. The color appears stronger while wet. For accurate results, allow the paper to dry completely.

3 ▼ Dip the various ends into the desired colors.

4 ▼ Carefully unfold the piece of paper and lay onto a scrap piece of paper. The dyed paper should dry completely before using as a covering material. Thinner tissue papers work best, but become more delicate once wet.

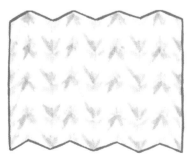

5 Once the paper is dry it may be used to cover board or be refolded into a new pattern to create a more complex design.

Gallery of Artist's Books

5 & 6

THE ARTISTS SHOWN HERE ARE FRIENDS and colleagues who choose to express themselves through the art of book and box making. Each of them contributes a great deal to the art world and I am honored to be able to represent their work in this book. Many of the examples shown are variations on the structures demonstrated in this book. Enjoy the images and build on some of their ideas to create innovative new structures of your own.

Andrew Borloz

Masu Boxes, 2006
3¹/₂" × 3¹/₂" × 1³/₄" (8.9 × 8.9 × 4.4 cm) largest box

The lid on each of the four *masu* boxes was folded from one piece of paper. The metallic patina was created by applying a mixture of acrylic paint and papier mâché paste with a silk sponge. A base coat was applied on the entire sheet and each layer of successive color was applied for depth. This technique was developed and taught by Jacqueline Sullivan (www.jacquelinesullivan.com). One of the lids was folded using the traditional Japanese method with a square piece of the paper, and the other lids are variations on the same method. However, some of the boxes require folding a rectangular piece into the final square shape before it becomes a lid. The bottom of each box is cut from card stock into a smaller size and folded using the traditional method. No adhesive was used in the creation of these simply elegant boxes.

Andrew Borloz has been folding and teaching origami as a volunteer for more than fifteen years. He was a former industrial designer and has more than six years of experience in consumer product design for manufacturers, and also has worked in exhibit design for museums and trade shows. He is involved in seeking various ways and techniques to alter the surface and appearance of paper for unique effects. His new company, Urban Paper Arts, LLC, was formed to provide classes and workshops in paper arts, book arts, art techniques, and mixed media.

www.urbanpaperarts.com
cooknfold@aol.com

Windows in Time, 2004
5¹/₂" × 3³/₄" (14 × 9.5 cm)

The pages of this unique book are ink-jet prints on papyrus. The text was written by the artist and sewn with the Ethiopian Coptic stitch with Coptic headbands. The covers are red leather with laced vellum, and they include on-lays, inlays, and blind tooling. Two slit braid leather loops and foredge pegs complete the closure.

Long Stitch Models, 2003
5" × 3" (12.7 × 7.6 cm)

These two books are covered in black calfskin. The spines are sewn on top of wooden back plates, one of which is cut from a measuring stick. A bone clasp and button keep the books closed.

Bonnie Stahlecker inspired my passion for book and box making. Bonnie was my first bookbinding instructor and influenced my binding education. I continue to use some of the original techniques shown to me so many years ago. Her appreciation of and commitment to making bound structures was a nurturing and logical step in my artistic development. Bonnie is a nationally recognized book artist who has taught and exhibited in many venues. Her work has been published in a number of books, including *Penland Book of Handmade Books*.

bstahlecker@sbcglobal.net

Emily Martin

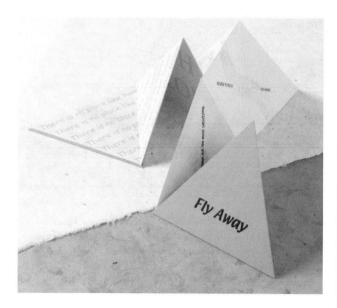

Fly Away, 2005
9" × 8" × 1" (22.9 × 20.3 × 2.5 cm)

This work is a triangular accordion book that was printed using letterpress, ink-jet, and pochoir on Japanese paper in an edition of fifty. The text muses on the desire to flee one's own life. A nontraditional variation of the Japanese double-leafed album, it includes an attached hard cover wrapped in colored Japanese paper.

Mutually Exclusive, 2002
6¼" × 4¼" (15.9 × 10.8 cm) each

A letterpress printed set of five magic wallets, provoked by the events of 9/11/01, which address the cacophony of news reports, emotions, analysis, and opinions that follow in the wake of any major news event. The righteous indignation and reciprocal intolerance whitewashed by ideals from religion to political correctness raise the question of personal belief. Using the magic wallet format, the book panels flip back and forth from two opposing statements, which reflect the slipperiness of forging a personal philosophy. Each of the texts has three layers, the large basic statements, an underlying stream-of-consciousness narration, and the ten sets from the Pythagorean table of opposites.

Emily Martin has been making artist's books since the late 70s. She earned an master of fine arts degree in painting from the University of Iowa in 1979. Since then Emily has been producing narrative paintings, sculpture, and books. Most of her earlier books were one-of-a-kind sculptural books. She began producing limited-edition books in the late 80s, using images from her paintings and drawings. In 1995, Emily created the Naughty Dog Press, producing books using text either alone or in combination with visual imagery. She uses a variety of printing methods with the books: ink-jet printing, letterpress, black-and-white and color photocopies, and offset. Her books are in public and private collections throughout the United States and internationally, including the Metropolitan Museum of Art, New York City; the Tate Gallery, London; the Museum of Contemporary Art of Chicago; the Walker Art Center, Minneapolis; the Marvin and Ruth Sackner Archive of Concrete and Visual Poetry, Miami Beach, Florida; and a number of educational institutions, including the Rhode Island School of Design, Harvard, Yale, and Wellesley College. Emily teaches at the University of Iowa Center for the Book and in workshops around the country.

www.emilymartin.com
emilyjmartin@mchsi.com

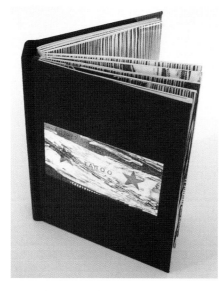

Tattoo, 2005
4⁵/₁₆" × 5¹/₄" × 1¹/₈" (11 × 13.3 × 2.9 cm)

This book features a woodcut with watercolor painted sections on each page. Various pop-ups come off of the page with every turn. The idea explores different tattoo ideas in conjunction with figurative elements from a larger print that was cut down to size.

Ticket Licket, 2001
10¹/₈" × 5³/₄" × ¹/₂" (25.7 × 14.6 × 1.3 cm)

A simple portfolio was created to house six individual double-sided reductive woodcut images. Reductive woodcuts are called *suicide prints* because the same block is used to print each color. Once the first color has been applied, the block is cut again to print any subsequent colors. Careful planning is needed, because once the image has been cut, there is no going back! *Ticket Licket* was inspired by raffle tickets that are commonly used as entrance into theme parks and benefits. The edition size was composed of seventy full portfolios.

www.benrinehart.com
ben_rinehart@yahoo.com

Leslie Koptcho

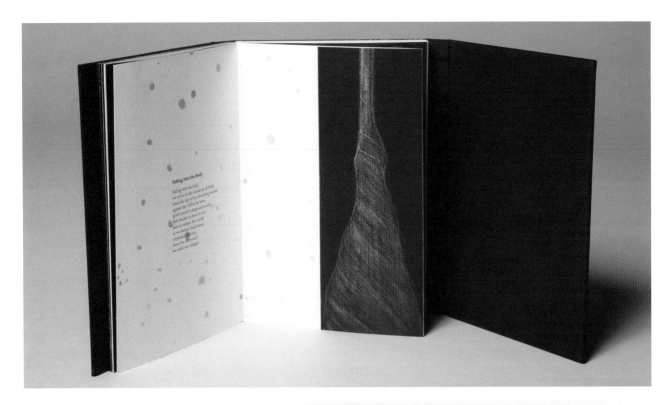

Falling Into, 1992
6¼" × 9" (15.9 × 22.9 cm)

This work is an editioned collaborative book work between the artist and designer Leslie Koptcho, the poet Ray Gonzalez, and the designer and typographer Rod Mills. The book is composed of color intaglios and letterpress printed pages. Leslie has been able to capture images of her own skin through the process of microscopy. Using both traditional light microscopes and scanning electron microscopes, she records images of her cells which are then digitally manipulated with computers and combined with hand-drawn, traditional processes. The result is a series of lithographs and etchings that explore the vast scientific concepts of evolution and intimate ideas of personal identity. Leslie's prints exist as both a diagram of the life of a species and of an individual.

Leslie Koptcho is a graduate of Cranbrook Academy of Art in Bloomfield Hills, Michigan. She teaches printmaking and book arts at Louisiana State University. Recent exhibitions of her work include the Kochi International Print Biennial in Seoul, Korea; the "Janet Turner National Print Exhibition" at the Janet Turner Museum in Chico, California; "Digital Louisiana" at the Contemporary Art Center in New Orleans; and "Next to S(k)in" at StoneMetal Press in San Antonio.

lkoptcho@lsu.edu

Leslie Koptcho & Kimberly Paul Arp

Pocket Baggage, 2001
2⁷/₈" × 4" × ¹/₂" (7.2 × 10.1 × 1.2 cm)

This is an editioned collaborative portfolio exchange between graduate students and faculty at Louisiana State University in Baton Rouge, directed by Leslie Koptcho. The group used the accordion structure with nontraditional materials such as wallet picture inserts to house each artist's print. Each image may be replaced and the order changed. The portfolio represents various printmaking and letterpress techniques and includes the following artists: Kimberly Arp, Alison Frank, Sara Hopp, Kathryn Hunter, Leslie Koptcho, Lori Penn, Andrew Saluti, Chris Stanley, and Jenny Swanson.

Kimberly Paul Arp received his master of fine arts degree in printmaking with distinction from Indiana University and has taught at the School of Art at Louisiana State University in Baton Rouge since 1977. He has had numerous solo exhibitions at the Aberdeen Art Gallery in Scotland, Joy Horwich Gallery in Chicago, Pelham Von Stoffler Gallery and McMurtrey Gallery in Houston, the University of Wisconsin, the University of Texas, the University of Arizona, Grays School of Art, and Peacock Printmakers in Aberdeen, Scotland, among others.

kimberlyarp@hotmail.com

Stephen Pittelkow

Assortment of Marbled Papers, 2005

These richly patterned, marbled papers were used on projects throughout the book. Using traditional techniques and contemporary color palettes, Steve's designs explode across the surface of the paper. Working on paper and cloth, his marbled designs have been used on numerous books and creative products. Steve's papers are in private and museum collections and his commissions include book artists, fine press binders, and graphic designers. He teaches marbling and bookbinding classes across the country and at Minnesota Center for Book Arts in Minneapolis, where he is also employed as the adult programs coordinator.

paperandbooks@mac.com

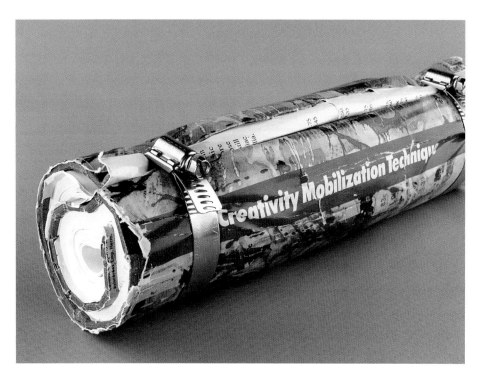

Book Implosion (Creativity Mobilization Technique), 2003
10" × 3" (25.4 × 7.6 cm) diameter

This one-of-a-kind book structure is made with a found book and hose clamps. Is the book dead? As we continue to make books, what function do they serve? Are they a useful means to convey and store information or will they become primarily aesthetic objects? With "Book Implosions," Edwin twists, folds, distorts, and clamps old textbooks, dictionaries, and manuals into objects that contain their original content but cannot be opened. With each piece, he seeks a method that forces the artifact to completely fold in on itself. The resulting sculpture remains to document the process of creating each unique book structure.

Book Implosion (First Course in Algebra), 2004
9" × 4" (22.9 × 10.2 cm) diameter

This one-of-a-kind book structure is made with a found book and hose clamps.

Edwin Jager is a print, book, and installation artist who has exhibited throughout the United States and Canada. He is an associate professor at the University of Wisconsin –Oshkosh. Edwin's passion for books is punctuated by his exhibition record, having many solo and group exhibitions focusing on prints and books as an expressive art form.

www.uwosh.edu/faculty_staff/jager/
jager@uwosh.edu

Hilary Lorenz

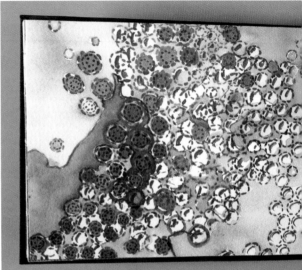

The Fragrance Grifters, 2005
5¹/₂" × 7³/₄" × ¹/₂" (14 × 19.7 × 1.3 cm)

A limited-edition, hand-created artist's book of hand-painted watercolors and poetry by Elaine Equi. All twelve pages are printed on medium weight watercolor paper imported from France. The cover is a silk cloth from Japan with a handprinted and flocked title. The pages were scanned and printed with an ink-jet printer using archival inks.

Hilary Lorenz received her master of fine arts degree in printmaking and multimedia from the University of Iowa. She has had numerous group and solo exhibitions throughout the United States, as well as in Europe and Asia. Hilary received a Fulbright Fellowship to Taiwan and has also received fellowships from the NEA Mid Atlantic Foundation; the Lower East Side Printshop's Special Collections Residency, New York City; the Frans Masereel Centrum's Printmaking Residency, Belgium; the Miskolc Museum of Contemporary Art Residency, Hungary; the School of the Art Institute of Chicago, Ox-Bow Artist Residency; the Manhattan Graphics; and the Robert Blackburn Printmaking Workshop, New York City. She created artwork and textile design for Merce Cunningham Dance Company. Her artwork has been reviewed in the *New York Times, Los Angeles Times, Art in America,* and *Art on Paper.*

www.hilarylorenz.com
hilary@hilarylorenz.com

Japanese Four-Drawer Box, 2004
1¹/₂" × 5" × 5" (3.8 × 12.7 × 12.7 cm)

This unique box has four drawers, one on each wall. Carolyn uses a variety of materials including screen-printed Japanese papers and book cloth.

Full Leather Decorative Box, 1998
5" × 2¹/₂" × 3¹/₂" (12.7 × 6.4 × 8.9 cm)

This one-of-a-kind box is created with binder's board and calfskin leather, and is tooled in gold.

Carolyn Chadwick has had the opportunity to hold extraordinary books, manuscripts, and prints. She once made a box for Edgar Allan Poe's spoon. She continues to work with many interesting collectors, publishers, artists, and bibliophiles. She binds small editions and presentation bindings, restores and rebinds older works, and makes boxes. Carolyn's customer list includes the New York Public Library, the Museum of Modern Art, Sotheby's, and many private collectors and artists.

Carolyn took her first bookbinding class in 1977 while working in the Rare Book Library at Columbia University in New York City. From that point she knew that a career devoted to the preservation and binding of books was a right fit. In 1978 she began training with master binder Mark Tomsett of the European Bookbinding Company in New York and continued working with him for twelve years. Carolyn began working on her own in 1990. She teaches at various institutions around the country, sharing her traditionally trained craft. Her goal is to share an appreciation for handcrafted quality binding to ensure it never disappears. Teaching provides her with stimulation and challenges from a wide variety of students.

Laurel Parker

Long Stitch Bindings, 2006
3³/₄" × 5³/₈" × ¹/₂" (9.5 × 13.7 × 1.3 cm) for each book.

These four sample bindings incorporate the long stitch sewn over dyed paper covers.

Laurel Parker studied fine arts at the School of the Museum of Fine Arts in Boston and at the Center for Book Arts in New York City, where she is currently a faculty member. Laurel lives and works primarily in Paris. After creating a series of artist's books for the Venice exhibition of *Ashes and Snow*, Laurel moved to Paris in 2003 to continue working with other artists. She founded her own studio in 2004 where she produces classical bindings, artists' books, journals, albums, and boxes, all one-of-a-kind or in small series. Her diverse clientele includes book collectors, artists, boutiques, businesses, and private clients.

www.laurelparkerbook.com
laurelparkerbook@hotmail.com

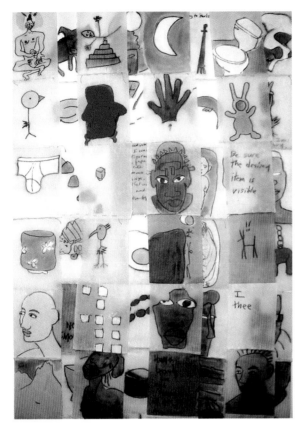

Little Things, 2003
52" × 68" (132.1 × 172.7 cm)

This is what Rory calls a hanging book. This one-of-a-kind book is composed of hand-sewn accordions that hang on the wall to form a composite image. The books collapse into a small stack and fit into a handmade box. The book shows myriad small drawings of childhood toys and memorabilia. The book was made by drawing with a pencil on handmade mulberry paper, painting the image, then applying a layer of beeswax to make the paper translucent. The books were then sewn with silk thread.

Texas Book, 2005
64" × 72" (162.6 × 182.9 cm)

This unique two-dimensional book hangs on the wall, but may also be folded into an accordion to fit into a box. The book was created on mulberry paper, embellished with gouache, charcoal, ink, and beeswax, and sewn with silk thread.

Rory Golden has owned and operated Palmapodoca Press, an independent fine press, since 1997. Rory publishes letterpress-printed broadsides of contemporary poetry, and limited-edition and one-of-a-kind artist's books. His paintings and books are exhibited nationally and are a part of many public and private collections around the country. Rory's solo exhibitions have been shown at the Bay Park Press in California, Fairmont State University in West Virginia, the New York Public Library Donnell Library Center, and the National Museum of Lesbian, Gay, Bisexual and Transgender History in New York City.

rorynewyork@hotmail.com

Rand Huebsch

Lexicon, 2005
7¹/₂" × 5" (19.1 × 12.7 cm)

For *Lexicon,* Rand Huebsch made miniature relief blocks by carving with a linoleum cutter into soft polymer blocks that are made of a similar material to white plastic erasers. The carved blocks were inked with a brayer (small roller), using oil-based etching ink. The blocks were printed by hand like rubber stamps. Greek mythology, medieval art, and ancient Middle Eastern carvings influenced the playful imagery.

Circe, 2005
5" × 8" × 9" (12.7 × 20.3 × 22.9 cm)

Circe is a tunnel book with four panels and hand-colored embossments. The accordion folded sides are printed with rubber stamps and water-based ink. To make Circe, Rand used uninked deeply etched copper plates, on an etching press, to emboss the black museum board. The nonimage areas of the panels were cut with a craft knife. Then the embossments were hand colored with water-soluble crayons, so that only the raised areas received the color and the recessed linear areas remained black.

Rand Huebsch is a printmaker and book artist, and creator of Parrhasia Press. His work is a part of the permanent collections at the Victoria and Albert Museum, London; the State Library of Queensland, Australia; the Detroit Institute of Arts; the Fogg Art Museum, Boston; and the New York Public Library. He cofounded the Manhattan Graphics Center in 1986 and has been a curator for printmaking shows at the New York Hall of Science. His technical articles have appeared in the British quarterly *Printmaking Today* and other publications.

www.randhuebsch.com

GLOSSARY

ACCORDION: folded sheet of paper, resembling a zigzag

ADHESIVE: natural or synthetic glue or paste used to adhere materials to one another

ARCHIVAL: term used for any product having a neutral pH or having no acid

AWL: tool used for punching through heavier materials or creating sewing stations

BACK SIDE: side of the material surface that is to be covered

BASE: bottom of a box, typically joined to the walls

BINDER'S BOARD: dense board used in creating hard covers and boxes

BONE FOLDER: tool used to fold, score, and tear

BOOK CLOTH: paper or starch-backed cloth used for covering binder's board

BURNISH: to rub or enhance an area with the use of a hand or tool

CASE: outside cover or housing for a book structure

CASING IN: gluing the text block into the cover or case

CHEATER'S STRIP: strip of board or metal used to compensate for the standard turn-in

COVER: the act of covering another material or a means of support or protection

COVER STOCK: a heavier paper used for covers and structures requiring more stability

COVERING MATERIAL: paper, cloth, or leather used to cover the binder's board

CRAFT KNIFE: tool used to cut through thinner materials

DECKLE: natural uneven edge of the paper, similar to a torn edge

DIVIDER: separation for boxes

END SHEET, END PAPER, FLY LEAF: typically paper that covers the turn-ins or joins the text block to the cover

FACE: nice or decorative side of the page or covering material

FOLIO: single sheet of paper folded in half

FOOT: see Tail

FOREDGE: portion of the book that is open, typically the opposite side or across from the spine edge

GUTTER: inside or the valley of a fold

HEAD: top of the book or box

HEADBAND: decorative or added support to the head of a book

HINGE: small strip of paper used to join two individual sheets together

KETTLE STITCH: a slipknot used in sewing to secure two signatures together

KNOCK UP or JOG: tapping and aligning loose paper so it is even

LEAF: single sheet or piece of paper

LINEN THREAD: strong archival thread used in sewing books together

METHYL CELLULOSE: a thin, clear archival adhesive

MICRO-SPATULA: thin metal tool used to reach hard-to-get-to places

MULL or SUPER: starched open-weave cheesecloth used for supporting a book or box

NEEDLES: tapestry, upholstery, or darner's needle used in sewing books together

OCTAVO: single sheet of paper folded three times

PASTE: natural or synthetic glue used to adhere materials to one another

PEAK: folded edge or top of a fold as it faces up, opposite of the gutter

PIN TOOL: tool used to punch sewing stations or create small holes

PLEXIGLAS: plastic version of glass, lighter in weight and semi-flexible

PVA (POLYVINYL ACETATE): heavy white archival adhesive

QUARTO: single sheet of paper folded twice

SECURING THE THREAD: action of making sure the thread does not fall off of the needle during sewing

SEWING STATION: hole created through which to sew

SCORE: compressing the fibers with a bone folder to aid in folding

SIGNATURE: gathering of folios, quarto, or octavo

SPINE: typically the sealed, sewn, or bound edge of a book or box

SPINE LINING: thin paper used to reinforce and keep the spine separate from the cover

SPRING DIVIDER: tool used as a caliper for repeated measurements

SQUARE: extra space around the cover, designed to protect the contents of the book or box. A term also used to determine a right angle as with cutting the materials

TAIL: bottom of the book or box

TEFLON FOLDER: plastic tool similar to the bone folder

TEXT BLOCK: the inside of a book

TIP ON: thin line of adhesive used to join two materials together

TURN-IN: portion of the covering material that covers the board on a book or box

UTILITY KNIFE: tool used to cut through heavier materials

VALLEY: see Gutter

WEAVER'S KNOT: a process of joining two individual threads together

SUPPLIERS & RESOURCES

USA

AIKO'S ART MATERIALS IMPORT, INC.
3347 North Clark Street
Chicago, IL 60657
773.404.5600
www.aikosart.com
aikosart@aol.com

BOOKMAKERS INTERNATIONAL LTD.
8260 Patuxent Range Road, Suite C
Jessup, MD 20794
301.604.7787
www.bookmakerscatalog.com
bookmakers@earthlink.net

COLOPHON BOOK ARTS SUPPLIES
3611 Ryan Street S.E.
Lacey, WA 98503
360.459.2940
www.home.earthlink.net/~colophon/
colophon@earthlink.com

DANIEL SMITH ARTISTS' MATERIALS
P.O. Box 84268
Seattle, WA 98124-5568
800.426.7923
206.223.9599
www.danielsmith.com
sales@danielsmith.com

DOLPHIN PAPERS
Murphy Art Center
1043 Virginia Avenue, Suite 2
Indianapolis, IN 46203
877.868.0002
317.822.3846
www.homepage.mac.com/
dolphinpapers
dolphinpapers@mac.com

HARCOURT BINDERY
51 Melcher Street
Boston, MA 02210
617.542.5858
www.harcourtbindery.com
info@harcourtbindery.com

NEW YORK CENTRAL ART SUPPLY, INC.
62 Third Avenue
New York, NY 10003
800.950.6111
212.473.7705
www.nycentralart.com
sales@nycentralart.com

TALAS
20 West 20th Street, 5th Floor
New York, NY 10011
212.219.0770
www.talasonline.com
info@talasonline.com

UNIVERSITY PRODUCTS
517 Main St.
Holyoke, MA 01041
800.628.1912
413.532.3372
www.universityproducts.com
info@universityproducts.com

AUSTRALIA

ARTWISE AMAZING PAPER
186 Enmore Road
Enmore, New South Wales 2042
61.02.9519.8237
www.amazingpaper.com.au
admin@amazingpaper.com.au

BIRDSALL LEATHER AND CRAFTS
36 Chegwyn Street
Botany, New South Wales 2019
61.02.9316.6299
www.birdsall-leather.com.au
info@birdsall-leather.com.au

PRIMROSE PARK ART AND CRAFT CENTRE
P.O. Box 152
Cremorne, New South Wales 2090
www.primrose-park.com.au
ppp@westnet.com.au

E.C. CHAPMAN AND CO. PTY. LTD.
60 Nepean Gorge Drive
P.O. Box 25
Mulgoa, New South Wales 2745
61.02.4773.8738

VICTORIAN BOOKBINDERS' GUILD
5 Dunsterville Street
Sandringham, Victoria 3191
61.03.9598.6076
http://home.vicnet.net.au/~bookbind

WILL'S QUILLS
1/166 Victoria Avenue
Chatswood, New South Wales 2067
61.02.9411.2500
www.cecilia-letteringart.com/ALL/
willsquills.html
wquills@fl.net.au

CANADA

THE JAPANESE PAPER PLACE
77 Brock Avenue
Toronto, Ontario M6K 2L3
416.538.9669
www.japanesepaperplace.com
washi@japanesepaperplace.com

LA PAPETERIE SAINT-ARMAND
3700 Rue Saint-Patrick
Montreal, Quebec H4E 1A2
514.931.8338
www.st-armand.com

PIERRE THIBAUDEAU
R.R.1, Grantley Road
Chesterville, Ontario K0C 1H0
613.448.1350

FRANCE

RELMA
3 Rue des Poitevins
75006 Paris
33.01.4325.4052
relma@wanadoo.fr

ROUGIER ET PLE
13-15 Boulevard des Filles
  du Calvaire
75003 Paris
33.0825.160.560
www.crea.tm.fr
commandes@artacrea.fr

GERMANY

DRUCKEN AND LERNEN
Bleicherstrasse 12
D-26122 Oldenburg
49.61.42.46478
www.drucken-und-lernen.de
drucher-wel-lernen@t-online.de

JOHANNES GERSTAECKER VERLAG
GMBH
Postfach 1165
D-53774 Eitorf
49.22.43.889.95
www.gerstaecker.de
bestellung@gerstaecker.com

PHILIPPINES

C AND J SPECIALTY PAPERS
(PHILS.), INC.
CJ Compound Bgy.
Langkiwa Binan
Laguna 4020
632.6700.8882
www.cnjpaper.com
cjsp@belltell.com.ph

QUILL
Level 3, Power Plant Mall
Rockwell Center
Amapola corner Estrella Streets
PI-1200 Makati City
632.898.1433
quill@lietz.com

SWEDEN

BOKBINDERIMATERIAL
Anders Strand
Gräsholmsvägen 12
SE-693 34 Degerfors
46.586.40.990

UNITED KINGDOM

THE FINE BINDERY
Bridge Approach
Mill Road
Wellingborough,
Northants NN8 1QN
44.01933.276689
sales@finebindery.fsnet.co.uk

J. HEWIT AND SONS LTD.
Kinauld Leather Works
Currie, Edinburgh EH14 5RS
44.0131.449.2206
www.hewit.com
sales@hewit.com

ABOUT THE AUTHOR

Benjamin D. Rinehart has lived in Brooklyn, New York, for many years. He offers workshops across the United States for children and adults on making books, boxes, and prints. Ben received his bachelor of fine arts degree from Herron School of Art in Indianapolis and his master of fine arts degree from Louisiana State University in Baton Rouge. He has taught in New York and New Jersey at Pratt Institute, Rutgers/Mason Gross School of the Arts, Fordham University, Long Island University, FIT, the Center for Book Arts, and Manhattan Graphics Center. Ben has been a visiting artist at many institutions across the United States including Pyramid Atlantic, Minnesota Center for Book Arts, San Francisco Center for the Book, and Brookfield Craft Center. In fall 2006 he joined the faculty at Lawrence University in Appleton, Wisconsin, as an assistant professor of art.

When Ben is not teaching, he is busy in his studio making art. He specializes in multimedia images with a strong focus on books, boxes, printmaking, drawing, and graphic design. His socially charged work is a part of many public and private collections around the country. He has exhibited nationally and internationally in numerous group and solo shows. For examples of his artwork and teaching schedule, visit his website at www.benrinehart.com.

ACKNOWLEDGMENTS

Who would have thought that after writing several articles I would take on such a challenging project and write my own book? I could not have done it without the help of my students, mentors, colleagues, and peers. I have been fortunate to work with so many wonderful people over the years. Each of them has assisted in making my teaching, and eventually this book, what it is today.

My thanks to my literary agent Judy Heiblum and my editor Mary Ann Hall for their commitment and support during this project.

Another thank-you goes to my mother Patricia, father James, sister Melissa, niece Sedona, and especially my twin sister, Aimee, for pushing me to do my best and creating endless challenges.

And lastly, I want to extend a special thanks to my partner Joshua Cobbs and our dog, Bubs, for loving me throughout the entire process. Joshua's calm demeanor and Bubs' tenacious personality continue to create a wonderful balancing effect in my life.